SOMATIC THERAPY 101

AN INTERACTIVE GUIDE TO ALLEVIATE STRESS, OVERCOME DEEP-ROOTED TRAUMA, AND STRENGTHEN THE MIND-BODY CONNECTION WITH EASY TOOLS AND EXERCISES (IN JUST 10 MINUTES A DAY)

LIZANNE DOUGLAS

CONTENTS

Get my **FREE** Yoga Bliss in 10 Minutes: Effortless Somatic Practices for Daily Wellness & **BONUS** Stress Symptom Checklist

Visit LizanneDouglas.com

Scan the QR with Your Phone Camera Below!

INTRODUCTION

Picture yourself on a long journey, trekking over mountains and through valleys. Even though there's so much beauty around you, it's difficult to appreciate it because you're carrying a heavy load— a backpack full of rocks. Each rock represents a stress or trauma you've experienced in your life—being verbally abused as a child, a miscarriage, or a failed marriage. The list goes on and on. Sometimes, you feel like you can't take another step. And then, one day, you stumble upon a revelation. You can set the backpack down. You don't have to carry the load ever again. Imagine the relief!

The transformative power of somatic therapy goes beyond addressing the rocks you're carrying and teaches you how to toss them away—once and for all. It equips you with tools to navigate your path with newfound lightness and clarity. Through the healing process, you will learn to reconnect with the beauty of your journey, fully embracing each moment without the weight of past burdens.

According to the National Counsel for Mental Wellbeing, 70% of all adults have experienced some type of traumatic event at least once in their lives. That's 223.4 million people walking around weighted down with rocks—each with their own story.

What's in *your* backpack? What past painful experiences are weighing *you* down? Maybe it's childhood abuse or neglect, a tragic accident, or even a dream that never came to life. Each rock looks different. They come in all shapes and sizes, and what is traumatic to one person might not be to another. What's most important is that you learn to identify and release what's bringing you down and holding you back.

Somatic therapy delves into the intricate connection between the mind and body, embracing a holistic approach to healing. This therapeutic method is founded on the principle that the body and mind are not separate entities but are deeply interconnected and influence each other. By focusing on this connection, somatic therapy offers a path to healing that goes beyond traditional therapy forms (like talk therapy), combining elements of psychotherapy with physical therapy to address a broad spectrum of ailments and conditions.

The scope of issues somatic therapy can address is broad, touching on mental health challenges such as stress, trauma, depression, and anxiety, as well as physical manifestations like chronic pain and illness. Its unique approach makes it particularly effective for individuals who have endured trauma, providing a pathway to process and release emotional distress that has been physically internalized. Moreover, it extends its benefits to a diverse group of individuals, including those grappling with addiction, athletes seeking to overcome performance blocks, performers aiming to enhance their expressive capabilities, and anyone else who may have unknowingly suppressed stress and emotions within their body.

At its core, somatic therapy works by raising awareness of bodily sensations and encouraging the exploration of how the body stores and manages stress and trauma. Through guided sessions, individuals learn to identify and tune into physical cues associated with emotional pain, gradually learning to release tension and restore bodily balance. This process not only aids in alleviating physical discomfort but also in mitigating the psychological impact of negative experiences. By re-establishing a healthy mind-body connection, somatic therapy empowers individuals to regain control over their emotional and physical well-being, leading to improved mental health, increased resilience, and a greater sense of peace.

The benefits of somatic therapy extend beyond immediate symptom relief, offering long-term tools and strategies for managing stress and emotional challenges. Participants often report enhanced self-awareness, improved emotional regulation, and a deeper understanding of the impact of past experiences on their present lives. This newfound insight enables individuals to navigate life's challenges with greater ease and confidence, fostering a sense of empowerment and autonomy in their healing journey.

In short, somatic therapy stands out as a dynamic and effective approach to healing that honors the profound connection between the mind and body. Addressing the physical symptoms of emotional pain opens the door to a more integrated and holistic path to wellness, appealing to a wide range of individuals seeking to overcome the burdens of past traumas and embrace a more fulfilling life.

The information you'll find in this book unveils a myriad of priceless benefits, offering transformative insights and practical pathways to enhance personal well-being and foster emotional resilience. This comprehensive guide illuminates the nuanced ways in which your body signals its needs and stored traumas, equipping you with a range of straightforward, actionable exercises tailored to liberate you from both physical and emotional burdens. You'll embark on a journey to mastering stress management and fine-tuning your nervous system, paving the way to a more tranquil and grounded existence.

By demystifying the principles of somatic therapy, this book lays out a clear, accessible roadmap complete with effective strategies and an extensive toolkit for adopting a body-centric approach to healing. It draws a clear distinction between the methodologies of somatic therapy and conventional talk therapy, enhancing your understanding of their unique benefits and how they complement one another.

Beyond just theoretical knowledge, this book empowers you to actively engage with and interpret bodily sensations, establishing a direct link to your emotional states. Additionally, it enriches your learning experience with exclusive access to a downloadable yoga course and guided companion meditations specifically created to support your journey toward achieving mental and physical equilibrium.

The information and exercises are designed to easily be incorporated into your everyday life, offering immediate and lasting solutions to improve your mind-body connection and elevate your overall emotional health. Whether you're looking to deepen your self-awareness, navigate life's challenges with greater ease, or simply cultivate a better relationship with your body, this book serves as your comprehensive guide to a more balanced and healthful existence.

The techniques outlined in this book are highlighted by the testimonies of transformations experienced by individuals from all walks of life, including notable figures and famous celebrities who have openly shared their journeys of healing and self-discovery. For instance, celebrities like Lady Gaga and Prince Harry have publicly discussed the benefits of somatic practices and therapy for managing their mental health and overcoming personal traumas. Lady Gaga, known for advocating mental health awareness, has credited somatic therapy for helping her navigate the challenges of fame and personal issues. Likewise, Prince Harry has talked about using therapeutic practices to deal with the loss of his mother and the pressures of royal life, emphasizing how these methods have offered him considerable relief and have prepared a pathway to emotional well-being.

These powerful endorsements highlight not just the universality of the book's core principles but also their practicality and potential to bring about meaningful change. Through their stories, we see the transformative impact of integrating body-oriented practices into one's life, providing both inspiration and tangible proof of the techniques' effectiveness.

Whether you're a public figure facing the glare of the spotlight or someone navigating the complexities of everyday life, the book offers a beacon of hope and a practical guide to achieving a more balanced and fulfilled state of being.

If you would like to explore somatic therapy even further on a personal level or are a clinician wishing to incorporate it into your practice, don't miss the next book in this series, *Somatic Therapy 201: Dive Deeper into the Mind-Body Connection with Advanced Tools to Master Self-Discovery and Growth.*

This book doesn't just provide a foundation for understanding the mind-body connection; it also opens the door to a world where self-care and mental health are intertwined with daily routines. By integrating these practices into your life, you gain the ability to turn everyday moments into opportunities for growth and healing. It's about turning knowledge into action, where the simple act of breathing deeply or moving intentionally can become a powerful tool for managing emotions and fostering well-being.

Before the accessibility of such resources, individuals often dealt with their mental and physical health on their own, relying on limited understanding and access to holistic practices. The integration of self-care and mental health into daily routines was not widely recognized, so many had no knowledge of these simple life-changing practices.

Beyond personal transformation, this book also offers a unique perspective on how somatic therapy can embrace and enhance interpersonal relationships. By becoming more attuned to your own body and emotions, you're better equipped to understand and empathize with others, enriching connections and fostering deeper bonds.

Embarking on this journey equips you with a holistic approach to wellness that transcends traditional methods of therapy. It's an invitation to live more fully, to embrace each moment with awareness and gratitude, and to discover the true peace that comes from being in harmony with your body and mind. This guide is not just about overcoming past traumas; it's about paving the way for a future where emotional resilience and physical health are the cornerstones of a life well-lived.

Perhaps most importantly, you'll have the opportunity to embark on an exciting journey of self-discovery, unveiling and getting acquainted with your authentic self in ways you might never have imagined. This process of uncovering the layers, recognizing your strengths, vulnerabilities, and the unique tapestry of your personal history, is not just enlightening—it's exhilarating. It offers a chance to reconnect with the core of who you are beyond the roles and expectations imposed by the world. Through this exploration, you'll find a deeper sense of purpose and a renewed passion for life, celebrating the true essence of your being with every step forward.

This book is for anyone who feels stuck and out of sync, who's been trying to heal but hasn't quite found the way, and for everyone who believes healing involves both the mind and the body. If you're ready to explore the teachings of somatic therapy with a personal touch and practical step-by-step mind-body exercise instructions, let's get started.

CHAPTER ONE

THE ESSENCE OF SOMATIC THERAPY

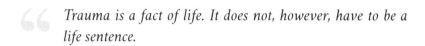

Trauma is a fact of life. It does not, however, have to be a life sentence.

— PETER A. LEVINE, SOMATIC EXPERIENCING® FOUNDER

On a quiet night in Ridgewood, New Jersey, a twenty-two-year-old college student named Lisa was taking her routine evening walk. As she was thinking about the next day's history exam and daydreaming about the guy who always sat next to her in class, she heard a sudden rustling in the tree line beside the sidewalk she was on. She wanted to run, but it was too late.

The attack was swift and merciless. Even though Lisa went through years of therapy, rehashing the incident over and over again, she never experienced freedom from it. Ten years later, she was still suffering from excruciating headaches and heart-pounding panic attacks. She found it difficult, if not impossible, to trust anyone. Her marriage was in total shambles. "It's like you're not even there," her husband told her. On the verge of divorce, she was determined to find answers.

That's when Lisa stumbled upon a therapist who introduced her to somatic therapy. It was a pivotal moment when she learned her body was housing the trauma she suffered so many years ago but that, through somatic therapy, it was possible to experience total recovery—mind, soul, and body. A light bulb went off in Lisa's mind. She was filled with hope and excitement because, finally, it was all beginning to make sense.

In this chapter, we'll explore the transformative potential of somatic therapy, weaving together the threads of age-old practices and cutting-edge research to discover how it can revolutionize our approach to wellness.

WHAT IS SOMATIC THERAPY?

As introduced earlier in this book, somatic therapy is a form of healing that taps into the wisdom of your body, a method that has been around since the dawn of humanity. This therapy, with its roots deeply embedded in our past, brings to the forefront solutions that are only now being recognized by modern science. More than a mere therapeutic technique, it takes you on a profound exploration of your innermost self—to reveal and embrace your authentic self.

So, how did somatic therapy all begin? Somatic therapy has deep historical roots dating back to ancient healing practices that recognized the interconnectedness of the mind and body through forms of bodywork, movement, and breathwork found in cultures worldwide, such as Ayurveda in ancient India, traditional Chinese medicine, and various indigenous healing traditions.

William Reich: In the early 20th century, Wilhelm Reich, an Austrian psychoanalyst and follower of Sigmund Freud, made significant contributions to somatic psychology. Reich developed the concept of character armor, suggesting that emotional experiences are stored in the body as muscular tension. He developed therapeutic techniques aimed at releasing this tension to address psychological distress. Reich's work laid the foundation for the understanding of the mind-body connection in psychotherapy.

Alexander Lowen: In the 1950s, Alexander Lowen, influenced by Reich's ideas, further developed somatic therapy through the creation of bioenergetic analysis. Lowen emphasized the importance of bodily expression and breathwork in releasing emotional trauma stored in the body. His approach integrated psychoanalytic theory with body-oriented techniques to address psychological and somatic issues.

Moshe Feldenkrais: Another key figure in the development of somatic therapy is Moshe Feldenkrais, who introduced the Feldenkrais Method in the mid-20th century. Feldenkrais believed in the capacity for individuals to improve their physical and emotional well-being through increased body awareness and movement re-education. His method focuses on gentle movements and self-awareness exercises to enhance physical functioning and emotional resilience.

Ida Rolf: Ida Rolf, a biochemist and the founder of structural integration (SI), also known as Rolfing, made significant contributions to somatic therapy in the 20th century. Rolf developed a systematic approach to manipulating the body's connective tissue to improve posture, movement, and overall well-being. Structural integration aims to realign the body's structure to alleviate physical discomfort and promote psychological integration.

Peter Levine: Peter Levine, the founder of Somatic Experiencing, further expanded somatic therapy in the late 20th century. His work focuses on resolving trauma by engaging the body's natural ability to self-regulate and heal. Somatic Experiencing emphasizes the importance of physical sensations and nervous system regulation in trauma resolution, offering a gentle and effective approach to healing traumatic experiences.

Stephen W. Porges: Stephen W. Porges is a notable figure in somatic therapy and is renowned for his work on polyvagal theory. His groundbreaking research highlights the critical role of the autonomic nervous system in regulating physiological and emotional responses to stress and trauma. Porges' Polyvagal Theory, a groundbreaking concept in neuroscience and psychology, proposing that the autonomic nervous system plays a crucial role in regulating social engagement, stress responses, and emotional states, has significantly influenced somatic therapy, informing innovative approaches aimed at restoring nervous system regulation and promoting healing from trauma. Therapists trained in Somatic Experiencing and other body-oriented modalities often integrate polyvagal-informed techniques into their practice to support clients in restoring a sense of safety, connection, and well-being.

Somatic therapy continues to evolve, combining insights from neuroscience, trauma research, and other therapeutic techniques. Today, somatic therapy encompasses a diverse range of approaches with unique perspectives that share a common emphasis on the body's role in processing and resolving trauma, promoting self-awareness, and enhancing overall well-being.

Somatic Experiencing

As mentioned above, Somatic Experiencing was developed by Dr. Peter A. Levine. Diving deeper, we learn that SE is a therapeutic approach focused on resolving trauma by addressing the physiological and emotional aspects of the nervous system's response to stress, recognizing that traumatic experiences can dysregulate the autonomic nervous system, leading to symptoms like hyperarousal, hypoarousal, and dissociation. Through gentle tracking of bodily sensations and the gradual release of trapped survival energy stored in the body, individuals learn to regulate their nervous system, establish safety, and integrate fragmented traumatic experiences, ultimately leading to healing and resilience.

Hakomi Therapy

Hakomi therapy, founded by Ron Kurtz in the 1970s, blends mindfulness, experiential psychotherapy, and body-centered techniques to explore and transform unconscious beliefs and patterns. Central to Hakomi is the concept of "mindfulness in assisted self-discovery," where therapists facilitate clients' exploration of present-moment experiences, including bodily sensations, emotions, and thoughts. Through gentle touch, movement, and dialogue, Hakomi helps access and reorganize neural networks associated with past trauma and limiting beliefs, fostering self-awareness, self-compassion, and profound shifts in perception and behavior.

Sensorimotor Psychotherapy

Sensorimotor psychotherapy, developed by Pat Ogden, integrates somatic psychology, attachment theory, and mindfulness practices to address trauma and attachment-related challenges. This approach recognizes the body as a primary resource for processing traumatic experiences and restoring a sense of safety and agency. By employing techniques like mindful movement, breathwork, and body-oriented interventions, sensorimotor psychotherapy helps clients regulate arousal levels, develop body awareness, and renegotiate traumatic memories stored in the body. Through exploring the interplay between bodily sensations, emotions, and cognitive processes, individuals can integrate fragmented experiences and cultivate greater wholeness and resilience.

Trauma Resiliency Model (TRM)

The trauma resiliency model, developed by Elaine Miller-Karas and Laurie Leitch, is a body-centered approach to trauma healing that focuses on building resilience and restoring balance in the nervous system. TRM emphasizes the importance of understanding the body's natural responses to stress and trauma, including the activation of survival instincts and the regulation of autonomic arousal. Through a combination of education, skill-building exercises, and somatic interventions, TRM helps individuals develop self-regulation skills, strengthen their capacity for resilience, and cultivate a sense of empowerment in navigating life's challenges.

Bioenergetic Analysis

Bioenergetic analysis, influenced by the work of Wilhelm Reich and further developed by Alexander Lowen, is a body-oriented psychotherapy approach that explores the interconnection between emotional experiences and bodily expressions. This method emphasizes the release of muscular tension and emotional blocks stored in the body, often through expressive movement, breathwork, and somatic exercises. By accessing and releasing unconscious patterns of holding and constriction, bioenergetic analysis aims to promote emotional release, enhance vitality, and facilitate psychological integration and growth.

Trauma-Informed Yoga

Trauma-informed yoga combines the principles of yoga with trauma-sensitive practices to support individuals in healing from traumatic experiences. This approach recognizes the potential triggers and challenges that traditional yoga practices may present for trauma survivors and adapts yoga techniques to create a safe and supportive environment. Trauma-informed yoga focuses on empowering individuals to reconnect with their bodies, regulate their nervous systems, and cultivate self-awareness and compassion. Through gentle movement, breath awareness, and mindfulness practices, trauma-informed yoga offers a holistic pathway to healing and resilience.This is discussed in more detail in Chapter 5.

Internal Family Systems (IFS)

Internal family systems therapy, developed by Richard Schwartz, is a non-pathologizing approach to psychotherapy that views the mind as composed of various sub-personalities or "parts." In IFS, therapists work with clients to identify and understand these internal parts, each with its own unique beliefs, emotions, and motivations. Through somatic techniques such as guided visualization, body scanning, and inner dialogue, individuals learn to access and communicate with their internal parts, fostering self-awareness, integration, and healing. IFS emphasizes the importance of cultivating self-compassion, curiosity, and curiosity toward all parts of the self, ultimately leading to greater emotional balance and wholeness.

Brainspotting

Brainspotting is a therapeutic approach that has gained significant attention in recent years for its effectiveness in treating trauma, emotional issues, and various psychological challenges. Developed by Dr. David Grand in 2003, brainspotting is based on the premise that eye positions can directly correlate with specific neural networks related to emotions, memories, and trauma stored in the brain. This therapy utilizes the client's field of vision to identify and access these neural networks, allowing for targeted processing and resolution of underlying issues.

Central to brainspotting is the concept of the "brainspot," which refers to a point in the client's visual field that corresponds with the activation of a specific neural network. These brainspots are identified through a process of guided attention and observation, often facilitated by the therapist using a pointer or the client's own gaze. Once a brainspot is identified, the therapist and client work collaboratively to explore and process the associated emotions, memories, or trauma.

One of the key advantages of brainspotting is its ability to access deep-seated emotions and memories that may be difficult to reach through traditional talk therapy alone. By bypassing the cognitive brain and directly engaging with the body's natural healing mechanisms, brainspotting can facilitate profound shifts in emotional and psychological well-being. Additionally, brainspotting is known for its gentle and noninvasive approach, making it suitable for individuals of all ages and backgrounds.

Brainspotting has been found to be particularly effective in treating trauma-related conditions such as post-traumatic stress disorder (PTSD), anxiety, depression, and dissociative disorders. Its flexibility and adaptability allow therapists to tailor the approach to meet the unique needs of each client, making it a versatile and powerful tool in the field of psychotherapy. As research and clinical evidence continue to support its efficacy, the technique is increasingly recognized as a valuable addition to the therapist's toolbox for promoting healing and transformation.

Biodynamic Psychotherapy

Biodynamic Psychotherapy is a holistic therapeutic approach that integrates principles from psychology, physiology, and energy dynamics to promote healing and well-being. Developed by Gerda Boyesen in the 1960s, biodynamic psychotherapy emphasizes the interconnectedness of the mind, body, and spirit, viewing mental and emotional health as intrinsically linked to the body's physiological processes.

Central to biodynamic psychotherapy is the concept of "biodynamic energy," which refers to the life force or vital energy that flows through the body. According to this approach, disruptions or blockages in the flow of biodynamic energy can manifest as psychological symptoms or emotional distress. Through a combination of verbal dialogue, body-centered techniques, and hands-on interventions, biodynamic psychotherapy aims to release tension, restore balance, and facilitate the natural healing process.

One of the distinguishing features of biodynamic psychotherapy is its emphasis on accessing and processing emotions stored in the body's tissues and organs. Therapists trained in this approach utilize a range of methods, including breathwork, gentle touch, and somatic awareness exercises, to help clients connect with and release unresolved emotional experiences.

Biodynamic psychotherapy recognizes the innate wisdom of the body and its capacity for self-regulation and healing. By creating a safe and supportive therapeutic environment, clients are encouraged to explore and express their emotions authentically, leading to greater self-awareness, resilience, and personal growth.

Overall, the technique offers a holistic and integrative approach to healing that addresses the interconnectedness of the mind, body, and spirit. With its emphasis on restoring balance and vitality to the whole person, it has the potential to bring about profound transformation and lasting well-being.

Resourcing

In somatic therapy, resourcing refers to the process of accessing internal and external supports to regulate the nervous system and enhance resilience. This may involve cultivating a sense of safety and grounding through breathwork, visualization, or connecting with supportive relationships and environments. By establishing resourcing practices, individuals can develop a greater capacity to navigate challenging experiences and regulate their emotions.

In somatic therapy, resourcing is not just about managing immediate distress; it also lays the foundation for long-term emotional well-being. By actively engaging with resourcing techniques, clients build a repertoire of skills that they can draw upon in various life situations. These skills extend beyond the therapy session, empowering individuals to respond to stressors with resilience and adaptability. Resourcing promotes a sense of agency and self-efficacy as clients learn to trust in their ability to navigate difficulties and cultivate a life of meaning and fulfillment. Through consistent practice and integration into daily life, resourcing becomes a cornerstone of holistic health and thriving.

These are good examples of the diverse range of somatic therapy techniques available, each offering its own unique perspective and approach to supporting individuals in their healing journey.

CORE PRINCIPLES OF SOMATIC THEORY

The core principles of somatic theory form the foundation of somatic therapy, guiding the process and empowering individuals on a journey of self-discovery, healing, and overall well-being. They are as follows:

Embodiment

The somatic theory emphasizes the importance of embodiment, recognizing that our bodies are not just vessels for our minds but integral aspects of our experience and identity. It acknowledges that our bodies store memories, emotions, and patterns of behavior and that addressing these physical manifestations is essential for healing and growth.

Body Awareness

Central to the somatic theory is the cultivation of body awareness —the ability to tune into and observe bodily sensations, emotions, and energy. This heightened awareness allows individuals to access valuable information stored within their bodies, gaining insights into their emotional state, triggers, and areas of tension or discomfort.

Sensory Motor Processing

The somatic theory highlights the intricate connection between sensory perception and motor responses. It recognizes that our nervous system continually processes sensory information from our environment and internal state, influencing our physical movements, behaviors, and emotional reactions. By understanding and working with this sensory-motor loop, somatic therapy aims to facilitate adaptive responses and restore equilibrium.

Trauma-Informed Approach

Somatic theory recognizes the pervasive impact of trauma on the body and psyche, emphasizing the need for trauma-informed care. It acknowledges that traumatic experiences can become stored in the body as physiological patterns of tension and dysregulation, contributing to a range of physical and emotional symptoms. Somatic therapy employs gentle, titrated interventions to support the gradual release and integration of trauma, promoting healing and resilience.

Mind-Body Integration

At its core, somatic theory advocates for the integration of mind and body, recognizing their inseparable nature. It emphasizes the bidirectional influence between thoughts, emotions, and bodily sensations, highlighting the role of the body as a gateway to deeper self-awareness and transformation. By fostering mind-body integration, somatic therapy facilitates holistic healing and alignment with one's authentic self.

DIFFERENTIATING SOMATIC THERAPY

Somatic therapy offers a distinct approach to healing that sets it apart from traditional therapy methods like talk therapy. Here's a detailed comparison highlighting the unique features of somatic therapy:

Integration of Body and Mind

Somatic therapy acknowledges the intimate connection between the body and mind, viewing them as interconnected aspects of the human experience. Unlike traditional therapy, which primarily focuses on verbal dialogue and cognitive processes, somatic therapy incorporates the body as an essential component of the healing process. Traditional therapy often relies on verbal communication to explore thoughts and emotions, while somatic therapy integrates bodily sensations, movements, and expressions to access deeper layers of experience and facilitate holistic healing.

Emphasis on Embodied Experience

Somatic therapy places a strong emphasis on embodied experience, recognizing that emotional issues and traumas are often stored in the body. By accessing and addressing these bodily sensations and patterns, somatic therapy allows individuals to process and integrate past experiences more effectively. In contrast, traditional therapy may overlook the somatic aspects of emotional distress, focusing primarily on cognitive insights and verbal expression. While talk therapy can be valuable for gaining insight and understanding, somatic therapy offers a more comprehensive approach that addresses the root causes of psychological symptoms at a somatic level.

Utilization of Body-Centered Techniques

Somatic therapy employs a variety of body-centered techniques to promote healing and self-awareness, such as breathwork, movement exercises, mindfulness practices, and touch-based interventions. These techniques facilitate the release of tension, regulation of the nervous system, and cultivation of embodied presence. Traditional therapy typically relies on verbal interventions such as interpretation, reflection, and analysis of thoughts and emotions. While these approaches can be insightful, they may not always address the somatic manifestations of psychological distress or trauma.

Expert Opinions

According to Dr. Peter Levine, founder of Somatic Experiencing, "Somatic therapy offers a pathway to healing that bypasses the limitations of traditional talk therapy by directly engaging the body's innate wisdom and capacity for self-regulation." Dr. Bessel van der Kolk, a renowned trauma expert, emphasizes the importance of somatic approaches in trauma treatment, stating that "Trauma is not just an event that took place sometime in the past; it is also the imprint left by that experience on mind, brain, and body." By integrating the body into the therapeutic process, somatic therapy provides a comprehensive and effective approach to healing that addresses the interconnected nature of physical, emotional, and psychological well-being.

THE SCIENCE OF MIND-BODY CONNECTION

When learning about somatic therapy—the essence of mind-body connection—it's imperative to realize it's not merely based on good ideas. There is science behind it. Lisa's headaches and panic attacks, that lump in your throat or racing heart you experience when something triggers a reminder of past trauma—those are all scientifically proven reactions resulting from the imprints of trauma.

The mind-body connection is a fundamental aspect of human experience, supported by extensive scientific research and studies. It involves the intricate interplay between psychological processes and bodily sensations, demonstrating how emotions can manifest physically and impact overall well-being.

Recent studies, such as those conducted at Washington University in St. Louis, have shed light on the neurological mechanisms underlying the mind-body connection. These studies suggest that the brain is intricately wired to integrate emotional experiences with bodily sensations, influencing various physiological responses. For example, when individuals experience stress, fear, or trauma, the brain initiates a cascade of physiological changes, leading to symptoms such as increased heart rate, muscle tension, and changes in breathing patterns.

Furthermore, research funded by the National Science Foundation has revealed the intricate pathways through which the mind and body communicate, highlighting the role of neural networks in mediating emotional and physical responses. These findings underscore the complexity of the mind-body connection and its profound implications for therapy and healing.

Physical Symptoms of Emotional Distress

Understanding the physical manifestations of emotional distress is crucial for recognizing the interconnectedness of mind and body in somatic therapy. Somatic symptoms refer to bodily sensations or experiences that arise in response to emotional or psychological distress, often manifesting as physical discomfort or dysfunction.

Somatic symptoms and related disorders encompass a wide range of physical complaints that may stem from underlying emotional issues. These symptoms are not merely psychosomatic (physical symptoms with no medical explanation, which are sometimes believed to be imaginary; they reflect genuine physiological responses to psychological stressors and traumas. Some common somatic symptoms and related disorders include:

Headaches and Joint Pains

Chronic headaches and joint pains are common manifestations of stress and emotional tension, often reflecting muscle tension and inflammation.

Stomach Aches and Nausea

Digestive disturbances, such as stomach aches and nausea, can occur in response to heightened anxiety or emotional distress, affecting gastrointestinal function.

Fatigue and Dizziness

Feelings of fatigue, weakness, and dizziness may result from prolonged stress or unresolved emotional trauma, impacting energy levels and overall well-being.

Memory Problems

Cognitive difficulties, including memory problems and difficulty concentrating, may arise as a result of chronic stress or psychological trauma, affecting cognitive function.

Trouble Breathing and Shortness of Breath

Respiratory symptoms, such as trouble breathing and shortness of breath, can occur during periods of intense anxiety or panic, leading to respiratory distress and hyperventilation.

Changes in Vision or Hearing

Emotional distress may manifest as changes in vision or hearing, including sudden blindness or auditory hallucinations, reflecting the impact of stress on sensory perception.

Feeling "Stuck" or a "Lump" in the Throat

Sensations of feeling "stuck" or having a "lump" in the throat are common somatic responses to emotional suppression or unresolved trauma, reflecting the constriction of throat muscles and difficulty expressing emotions.

Seizure-Like Episodes and Fainting

In extreme cases, emotional distress can manifest as seizure-like episodes or fainting spells, reflecting dysregulation of the autonomic nervous system and impaired stress response.

Overall, understanding the physical symptoms of emotional distress is essential for comprehensive assessment and treatment in somatic therapy, as it allows therapists to address underlying psychological issues and promote holistic healing of the mind and body.

INTERACTIVE ELEMENT

Incorporating reflective journaling prompts can deepen readers' engagement with the material and encourage self-reflection on their perceptions of somatic therapy and the mind-body connection. Consider the following journal prompt:

Reflective Journal Prompt

Recall a recent experience when you encountered a strong emotion, such as joy, anger, sadness, or fear. Take a moment to remember the circumstances surrounding this emotion and how it impacted you physically. Did you notice any specific sensations or changes in your body, such as muscle tension, increased heart rate, shallow breathing, or butterflies in your stomach?

Now, contemplate the connection between your emotional experience and these bodily sensations. How do you interpret this interplay between your mind and body? Do you believe that your emotional state can influence your physical well-being and vice versa? Reflect on any insights or realizations that arise from exploring this connection.

Take your time with this exercise, and allow yourself to delve deeper into your thoughts and feelings. Remember, journaling is a powerful tool for self-exploration and can provide valuable insights into your inner world and the mind-body connection.

FINAL THOUGHTS

In this chapter, we delved into the profound world of somatic therapy and the intricate connections between our minds and bodies. From exploring its historical roots to understanding its core principles, we've gained valuable insights into how somatic therapy offers a holistic approach to healing and self-discovery.

As we reflect on the science of the mind-body connection, it becomes evident that our emotions and physical sensations are deeply intertwined. Through scientific studies and personal reflections, we've witnessed how trauma and emotional distress can manifest in physical symptoms, highlighting the importance of addressing both mental and physical aspects in therapy.

Now, armed with a deeper understanding of somatic therapy and the mind-body connection, it's time to put these insights into action. Consider continuing to journal about your own experiences with emotions and physical sensations, as discussed in the interactive element. By exploring these connections within yourself, you can cultivate greater self-awareness and pave the way for healing and growth.

Looking ahead, our journey continues into the realm of the connection between stress and the body. We'll learn how stress and trauma reside not just in our minds but are deeply woven into the fabric of our bodies. Get ready to uncover the language of the body and discover how understanding this language can lead to profound healing and self-awareness. Stay tuned for an exploration of the intricate interplay between stress, trauma, and the body's innate wisdom.

CHAPTER TWO

THE STRESS-BODY CONNECTION

Have you ever heard the phrase "stress is a killer?" While it may sound like a cliché, the truth behind these words is far more profound than many realize. In this chapter, we'll unravel the intricate relationship between stress and the body, exploring how this silent assailant not only impacts our physical health but also infiltrates every aspect of our well-being.

UNDERSTANDING STRESS

Stress is a silent assassin—far more than just a fleeting feeling of pressure or tension; it's a silent assassin that lurks beneath the surface, wreaking havoc on our bodies and minds. From high blood pressure to weakened immune systems, the physiological toll of stress is well-documented and often alarming. But its reach extends far beyond the confines of our physical health, with devastating effects.

Stress not only kills vitality and joy but also dreams, peace of mind, and aspirations. The toll of stress extends beyond the physical realm, infiltrating our mental and emotional well-being with ruthless efficiency. The good news is that through somatic therapy, we can reclaim all that stress has stolen from us.

There are three types of stress that impact the body in different ways. These include acute stress, chronic stress, and traumatic stress. Stress manifests in various forms, each exerting a unique toll on our physical and mental well-being. Understanding these different types of stress is crucial for effectively managing its effects on the body.

- **Acute Stress:** This type of stress is short-term and often triggered by immediate threats or challenges, such as a looming deadline or a sudden argument. While acute stress can be intense, the body typically returns to a state of equilibrium once the stressor is removed. However, repeated exposure to acute stressors without adequate recovery can contribute to chronic stress and its associated health issues.
- **Chronic Stress:** Chronic stress occurs when individuals experience prolonged periods of stress without relief or resolution. This type of stress is often linked to ongoing life challenges such as financial problems, relationship issues, or work-related pressures. Unlike acute stress, which subsides relatively quickly, chronic stress can persist for weeks, months, or even years, taking a significant toll on physical and mental health.
- **Traumatic Stress**: Traumatic stress results from exposure to traumatic events or experiences that pose a threat to life or well-being. Examples include natural disasters, accidents, physical or sexual assault, or witnessing

violence. Traumatic stress can have profound and long-lasting effects on the body, leading to conditions such as post-traumatic stress disorder (PTSD) and contributing to a range of physical health problems.

Effects of Stress on the Body

Regardless of the type, stress triggers a cascade of physiological responses that can have far-reaching effects on the body. When faced with a stressor, the brain activates the sympathetic nervous system, initiating the fight-or-flight response. This response triggers the release of stress hormones like cortisol and adrenaline, which prepare the body to respond to the perceived threat.

While the fight-or-flight response is crucial for survival in dangerous situations, chronic activation of this stress response can wreak havoc on the body. Prolonged exposure to stress hormones can lead to a range of health issues, including:

- Cardiovascular problems such as high blood pressure, heart disease, and stroke.
- Immune system suppression increases susceptibility to infections and illnesses.
- Digestive disorders like irritable bowel syndrome (IBS) and gastroesophageal reflux disease (GERD).
- Mental health issues, including anxiety, depression, and PTSD.

Understanding the physiological impact of stress is essential for implementing effective stress management strategies and promoting overall well-being. By recognizing the signs of stress and adopting healthy coping mechanisms, individuals can mitigate its harmful effects and cultivate resilience in the face of life's challenges. There are three stages of stress which include:

- **Alarm Stage:** Initiated by the perception of a threat, whether real or imagined, the body swiftly activates its sympathetic nervous system. This rapid response floods the bloodstream with stress hormones like adrenaline and cortisol, setting off a cascade of physiological changes. Heart rate escalates, blood pressure spikes, and senses sharpen, preparing the body for immediate action. Nonessential functions take a back seat as the body prioritizes survival-related processes.
- **Resistance Stage:** As the stressor persists, the body enters a phase of adaptation known as the resistance stage. Here, the body strives to maintain equilibrium amid ongoing stress, orchestrated by the hypothalamic-pituitary-adrenal (HPA) axis. Cortisol levels remain elevated, bolstering energy reserves and aiding in coping with prolonged stress. While outwardly functioning, prolonged exposure to stress can gradually wear down the body's systems, heightening the risk of chronic health issues and psychological strain.
- **Exhaustion Stage:** Stress should endure unabated, and the body eventually succumbs to the exhaustion stage. Resources become depleted, and physiological functioning falters, signaling a breakdown in resilience. Prolonged exposure to stress hormones takes its toll, leading to immune suppression, inflammation, and cardiovascular complications. Symptoms of exhaustion manifest as overwhelming fatigue, emotional burnout, and increased vulnerability to illness.

IDENTIFYING STRESS SYMPTOMS

Recognizing the signs of stress and anxiety is crucial for managing one's well-being effectively. Here, we'll delve into common physical symptoms, self-observation techniques, and practices for body acceptance.

Common Physical Symptoms

Stress and anxiety can manifest in various physical ways, including muscle tension, headaches, fatigue, and digestive issues. These symptoms serve as signals from the body, indicating underlying stressors that require attention and care.

Self-Observation Techniques

Developing self-awareness is key to identifying stress symptoms early on. Techniques such as mindfulness and self-reflection can help individuals observe their thoughts, emotions, and bodily sensations without judgment. By tuning into the body's signals, individuals can gain insight into their stress levels and take proactive steps to address them.

- **Change Your Stinkin' Thinkin':** If you feel your emotions spiraling downward, you can replace negative thoughts (such as "I'm a loser") with positive attributions. In doing so, you'll separate your feelings from facts, which will, in turn, produce more favorable, productive results and a more positive self-image.
- **Practice Gratitude:** Take time each day to reflect on things you're grateful for. Cultivating a gratitude practice can shift your focus away from stressors and promote feelings of positivity and well-being.

- **Engage in Physical Activity**: Incorporate regular physical activity into your routine to help reduce stress and boost mood. Exercise releases endorphins, which are natural mood lifters, and can help you feel more energized and resilient in the face of stress.
- **Connect with Nature**: Spend time outdoors and immerse yourself in nature. Whether it's taking a walk in the park, gardening, or simply sitting outside and enjoying the fresh air, connecting with nature can have a calming and rejuvenating effect on the mind and body.
- **Body Acceptance Practices:** Body acceptance involves embracing and honoring the body's natural form, regardless of societal norms or standards. It goes beyond body positivity, focusing on cultivating a compassionate and nonjudgmental relationship with one's body. Here are some practices to foster body acceptance:
- **Start with Body Neutrality**: Shift focus from appearance to function, appreciating the body's capabilities and strengths.
- **Watch Your Social Media Feeds**: Curate a positive online environment by following accounts that promote body diversity and acceptance.
- **Connect with the Present Moment**: Practice mindfulness to anchor yourself in the present moment and cultivate gratitude for your body's sensations.
- **Trust Your Body**: Listen to your body's cues and honor its need for rest, nourishment, and movement.
- **Notice What You're Grateful For**: Cultivate a gratitude practice, acknowledging the ways in which your body supports you each day.
- **Put the Body Feels First:** Prioritize activities that promote physical well-being and comfort, such as gentle movement, relaxation, and self-care.

- **Keep Your Gaze Outward Too:** Focus on contributing to the world in meaningful ways beyond appearance, emphasizing qualities such as kindness, empathy, and creativity.

Managing Stress

If you don't manage stress, it will manage you. Action is required. Here are some practical strategies to manage stress and promote overall well-being supported by scientific evidence:

- **Get Regular Physical Activity:** Engage in physical exercise on most days of the week. Exercise stimulates the production of endorphins, neurotransmitters that act as natural painkillers and mood elevators. Research has shown that regular physical activity can reduce symptoms of anxiety and depression, enhance mood, and improve overall well-being.
- **Practice Relaxation Techniques:** Incorporate relaxation techniques such as deep breathing, progressive muscle relaxation, or meditation into your daily routine. These practices activate the body's relaxation response, reducing levels of stress hormones like cortisol and promoting feelings of calm and relaxation.
- **Maintain a Sense of Humor:** Find moments of laughter and levity in your daily life. Laughter triggers the release of endorphins and promotes relaxation, reducing levels of stress hormones. Studies have shown that humor therapy can improve mood, reduce stress, and enhance overall quality of life.
- **Spend Time with Loved Ones:** Foster connections with family and friends. Social support has been linked to lower levels of stress and greater resilience in the face of

adversity. Spending time with loved ones can provide emotional support, encouragement, and a sense of belonging, all of which contribute to overall well-being.

- **Pursue Hobbies and Interests**: Set aside time for activities that bring you joy and fulfillment. Engaging in hobbies and interests can distract from stressors, promote feelings of mastery and accomplishment, and provide a sense of purpose and meaning in life.
- **Journaling**: Write in a journal to express your thoughts, feelings, and experiences. Journaling can help you gain insight into your emotions, identify sources of stress, and develop coping strategies. Research suggests that expressive writing can reduce symptoms of stress, anxiety, and depression and improve overall psychological well-being.
- **Prioritize Sleep**: Ensure you get enough restful sleep each night. Adequate sleep is essential for physical and mental health, including stress management. Sleep deprivation can impair cognitive function, increase irritability and mood disturbances, and exacerbate stress levels. Aim for 7–9 hours of sleep per night to support optimal well-being.
- **Eat a Healthy Diet**: Fuel your body with nutritious foods that support overall health. A balanced diet rich in fruits, vegetables, whole grains, and lean proteins provides essential nutrients that support stress resilience and overall well-being. Avoiding excessive caffeine, sugar, and processed foods can help stabilize mood and energy levels.
- **Avoid Harmful Substances**: Minimize or eliminate the use of tobacco, alcohol, and illicit drugs. These substances can magnify stress, anxiety, and depression and have detrimental effects on physical and mental health. Making

healthy lifestyle choices can help reduce stress levels and promote long-term well-being.

Incorporating these evidence-based strategies into your daily routine can help you effectively manage stress and cultivate a greater sense of well-being. By prioritizing self-care and adopting healthy habits, you empower yourself to navigate life's challenges with resilience and vitality.

Self-Observation

Self-observation is a fundamental practice in self-awareness and personal development, involving the intentional and mindful examination of one's thoughts, feelings, behaviors, and experiences. Through self-observation, individuals cultivate a deeper understanding of themselves, gaining insight into their patterns, tendencies, strengths, and areas for growth. This process often begins with a curious and nonjudgmental attitude, allowing individuals to observe themselves with openness and acceptance.

Furthermore, self-observation serves as a gateway to self-regulation and transformation. By becoming more attuned to their internal experiences, individuals can identify triggers, reactions, and underlying emotions that influence their behavior and decision-making. This awareness provides the opportunity to pause, reflect, and choose intentional responses rather than reacting impulsively or unconsciously. Over time, consistent self-observation fosters greater self-control, emotional intelligence, and the ability to navigate life's challenges with resilience and grace.

Self-observation is not limited to looking inward but also extends to the external world. It involves paying attention to the interactions, dynamics, and feedback received from others, as well as the impact of environmental factors on one's well-being. By integrating both internal and external observations, individuals gain a holistic understanding of themselves and their surroundings, empowering them to make informed choices and live in alignment with their values and aspirations.

Level 1 self-observation involves developing awareness of one's thoughts, feelings, and bodily sensations without judgment or interpretation. It's about observing the present-moment experience as it arises and accepting it for what it is without getting caught up in analysis or reaction. This level of self-awareness lays the foundation for deeper introspection and personal growth, serving as a starting point for cultivating mindfulness and understanding one's inner landscape.

At level 2 of self-observation, individuals may deepen their exploration beyond surface-level thoughts and emotions to uncover subconscious patterns and beliefs that shape their behavior. This stage involves delving into the underlying motivations, fears, and desires that influence one's actions, allowing for a more profound understanding of oneself. Level 2 self-observation encourages individuals to confront and address deeply ingrained patterns that may be hindering personal growth, leading to greater self-awareness and transformative insights.

Ultimately, self-observation can be on a lighter or deeper level. It is a lifelong practice that cultivates self-awareness, empowerment, and personal growth, laying the foundation for a fulfilling and meaningful life journey.

SOMATIC THERAPY FOR STRESS MANAGEMENT

At the heart of somatic therapy are somatic exercises, which play a crucial role in managing stress and enhancing mental health. These exercises encompass a wide range of practices aimed at promoting body awareness, mindfulness, and relaxation. They engage both the body and the mind, helping you release tension, reduce stress, and cultivate a deeper connection with yourself. While the concept of somatic therapy dates back centuries, the modern understanding and application of somatic exercises have evolved significantly, drawing from scientific research, psychological theory, and traditional healing practices.

Mindfulness, a key component of somatic therapy, involves paying deliberate attention to the present moment without judgment. By cultivating mindfulness, you can develop a greater awareness of your thoughts, emotions, and bodily sensations, allowing you to respond to stressors more effectively and with greater resilience. Body awareness, another fundamental aspect of somatic therapy, involves tuning into the physical sensations and signals of the body, such as muscle tension, breath patterns, and posture. By honing your body awareness, you are able to identify and address sources of stress and tension in your body, promoting relaxation and overall well-being.

Together, somatic exercises, mindfulness, and body awareness form a powerful toolkit for managing stress and improving mental health. These practices empower you to cultivate a deeper understanding of yourself, develop healthier coping strategies, and foster a greater sense of balance and resilience in the face of life's challenges.

Let's put what we've learned into practice with the somatic exercise techniques below:

Grounding Exercises

5, 4, 3, 2, 1

Grounding exercises are simple yet effective techniques to calm anxiety and bring yourself back to the present moment. One such exercise is the "5, 4, 3, 2, 1" coping technique for anxiety. Before beginning this exercise, take a moment to focus on your breathing, taking slow, deep breaths to help center yourself.

Step 1: Acknowledge Five Things You See (Duration: 1 minute)

Take a moment to look around and identify five things you see in your immediate surroundings. It could be anything from objects in the room to nature outside the window. Take your time to notice each item and mentally acknowledge its presence.

Step 2: Acknowledge Four Things You Can Touch (Duration: 1 minute)

Next, focus on your sense of touch and identify four things you can physically touch around you. It could be the fabric of your clothing, the texture of a nearby surface, or the sensation of the ground beneath your feet. Take a moment to feel each object and notice its tactile qualities.

Step 3: Acknowledge Three Things You Hear (Duration: 1 minute)

Shift your attention to your sense of hearing and identify three things you can hear in your environment. It could be the sound of traffic outside, the hum of electronics, or the rustling of leaves.

Focus on external sounds that you can hear beyond your own body.

Step 4: Acknowledge Two Things You Can Smell (Duration: 1 minute)

Bring your awareness to your sense of smell and identify two things you can smell nearby. It could be the scent of food cooking, the fragrance of flowers, or the aroma of a familiar object. Take a moment to inhale deeply and notice the distinct smells around you.

Step 5: Acknowledge One Thing You Can Taste (Duration: 1 minute)

Finally, focus on your sense of taste and identify one thing you can taste in your mouth. It could be the lingering flavor of a recent meal, the taste of toothpaste, or the freshness of water. Take a moment to notice the sensation of taste on your palate.

By completing these grounding exercises, you can bring yourself back to the present moment and alleviate feelings of anxiety or overwhelm. Remember to take your time with each step and focus on engaging your senses fully.

Breathwork

Breathwork, a scientifically proven method, harnesses the power of controlled breathing to regulate the body's stress response and promote relaxation.

Step-by-Step Breathwork Exercise

Step 1: Find a Comfortable Position

Sit or lie down in a comfortable position where you can relax without any distractions. You can close your eyes if you feel comfortable doing so.

Step 2: Relax Your Body

Take a few moments to scan your body and release any tension you may be holding. Start from the top of your head and work your way down to your toes, consciously relaxing each part of your body.

Step 3: Focus on Your Breath

Begin to focus your attention on your breath. Notice the sensation of the air entering and leaving your nostrils or the rise and fall of your chest and abdomen.

Step 4: Deep Breathing

Take a deep breath through your nose, allowing your abdomen to expand fully. Hold your breath for a moment, then exhale slowly through your mouth, allowing your abdomen to contract. Repeat this deep breathing pattern several times, allowing each breath to become slower and more relaxed.

Step 5: Counting Your Breath

As you continue to breathe deeply, you may find it helpful to count your breaths. Inhale slowly to the count of four, hold for a count of four, and exhale slowly to the count of four. Repeat this four-count breathing cycle several times, allowing yourself to relax more deeply with each breath.

Step 6: Notice Your Thoughts

As you breathe, you may notice thoughts or distractions arising in your mind. Instead of trying to push these thoughts away, simply acknowledge them and gently return your focus to your breath.

Step 7: Lengthen Your Exhalation

As you become more comfortable with the deep breathing pattern, you can experiment with lengthening your exhalation. Try inhaling to the count of four and exhaling to the count of six or eight. Lengthening the exhalation can help to further calm the nervous system and promote relaxation.

Step 8: Continue for Several Minutes

Continue with the deep breathing and counting for several minutes, allowing yourself to sink deeper into relaxation with each breath.

Step 9: Transition Slowly

When you are ready to end the breathwork exercise, gradually transition back to your normal breathing pattern. Take a few deep breaths, wiggle your fingers and toes, and slowly open your eyes.

Step 10: Reflect

Take a moment to reflect on how you feel after completing the breathwork exercise. Notice any changes in your body, mind, or emotions, and appreciate the sense of calm and relaxation you have cultivated.

Other Types of Somatic Exercises

- **Somatic Experiencing:** Somatic Experiencing is a body-oriented approach to healing trauma. It focuses on releasing the physical tension and sensations associated with traumatic experiences. During a session, a trained therapist guides the individual to track bodily sensations, allowing them to gradually process and release trapped energy from past trauma. Instructions may involve bringing attention to physical sensations, such as tension or relaxation, and gently exploring any emotions or memories that arise.

- **Eye Movement Desensitization and Reprocessing (EMDR):** EMDR is a psychotherapy technique and excellent diagnostic tool used to alleviate distress associated with traumatic memories. It involves recalling distressing memories while simultaneously focusing on external stimuli, typically the therapist's hand movements or auditory cues. This dual focus is thought to help desensitize the individual to the traumatic memory, reducing its emotional impact. Instructions typically involve following the therapist's hand movements or auditory cues while allowing thoughts and feelings to arise and pass.

- **Dance:** Dance therapy involves using movement and dance as a form of expression and healing. It allows individuals to connect with their bodies, release pent-up emotions, and explore self-expression in a safe and supportive environment. Instructions may include guided movements or improvisational dance, encouraging individuals to tune into their bodily sensations and emotions while moving freely.

- **Sensorimotor Psychotherapy**: As mentioned before, sensorimotor psychotherapy integrates mindfulness, body awareness, and movement to address trauma and emotional distress. It focuses on how the body holds and processes traumatic experiences, aiming to release tension and promote healing. Instructions may involve gentle movement exercises, mindfulness practices, and somatic awareness techniques to help individuals regulate their nervous system and deepen their connection to their bodies and emotions.

Real-Life Case Studies

Let's look at some real individuals who have successfully managed stress through somatic therapy.

John's Journey through Grounding Exercises

John, a thirty-five-year-old marketing executive, sought therapy to address his chronic anxiety and feelings of overwhelm. Despite his professional success, John struggled with persistent worrying thoughts and difficulty focusing on the present moment. His therapist, Dr. Smith, recognized the importance of grounding exercises in helping John manage his symptoms and guided him through a series of techniques aimed at increasing his present-moment awareness.

During their sessions, Dr. Smith explained to John the concept of grounding and its significance in managing anxiety. She emphasized that grounding techniques help individuals reconnect with the present moment by engaging their senses and shifting their focus away from anxious thoughts. Dr. Smith further explained the neuroscience behind grounding, highlighting the three compartments of the brain involved in processing information:

the reptilian brain (or basal ganglia), the limbic system (including the amygdala), and the neocortex.

The reptilian brain, also known as the basal ganglia, is responsible for regulating basic survival functions and instinctual behaviors. It operates on autopilot, controlling essential functions such as breathing, heart rate, and movement. The limbic system, which includes structures like the amygdala, plays a central role in processing emotions and memories. It helps evaluate threats and triggers the body's stress response when faced with perceived dangers. Lastly, the neocortex is the most evolved part of the brain, responsible for higher-order thinking, rational decision-making, and self-awareness.

Dr. Smith explained to John that chronic anxiety often stems from overactivation of the limbic system, which can hijack the brain's attention and keep individuals stuck in a cycle of worry and fear. By engaging in grounding exercises, individuals like John can redirect their focus to the present moment, bypassing the overactive limbic system and accessing the neocortex's rational problem-solving abilities.

John quickly grasped the importance of grounding and began incorporating these techniques into his daily routine. He practiced mindfulness exercises, such as deep breathing and sensory awareness, whenever he felt overwhelmed or anxious. Through consistent practice, John noticed a significant reduction in his anxiety symptoms and an increased ability to stay present in challenging situations.

As John continued his therapy journey, he gained a deeper understanding of the interconnectedness between mind and body and the power of grounding exercises in promoting emotional wellbeing. By embracing the present moment and learning to quiet his racing thoughts, John found a newfound sense of calm and resilience in navigating life's stressors.

Emily's Exploration of Mindfulness

Emily, a 42-year-old accountant, sought therapy to address her persistent feelings of sadness and dissatisfaction with life. Despite her professional success and stable family life, Emily struggled with a sense of emptiness and disconnection. Her therapist, Dr. Patel, recognized the potential benefits of mindfulness practices in helping Emily cultivate a deeper sense of presence and contentment.

During their sessions, Dr. Patel introduced Emily to the concept of mindfulness and its role in promoting emotional well-being. She explained that mindfulness involves intentionally focusing on the present moment with openness, curiosity, and acceptance. Dr. Patel emphasized that mindfulness practices can help individuals like Emily develop greater self-awareness, regulate their emotions, and cultivate a more compassionate attitude toward themselves and others.

Dr. Patel also discussed the neuroscience behind mindfulness, highlighting the brain's ability to change and adapt through neuro-plasticity. She explained that regular mindfulness practice can lead to structural and functional changes in the brain, including increased activity in regions associated with emotional regulation and decreased activity in areas linked to rumination and stress.

For Emily, mindfulness offered a way to break free from the grip of her negative thought patterns and cultivate a greater sense of peace and fulfillment. Dr. Patel guided Emily through various mindfulness exercises, including mindful breathing, body scan meditations, and loving-kindness practices.

As Emily began integrating mindfulness into her daily life, she noticed subtle shifts in her mindset and overall well-being. She became more attuned to her thoughts and emotions, allowing her to respond to life's challenges with greater clarity and resilience. Over time, Emily developed a deeper sense of gratitude for the present moment and a newfound appreciation for the simple joys in life.

Through her journey with mindfulness, Emily discovered a powerful tool for transforming her relationship with herself and the world around her. By embracing mindfulness as a way of life, she found the peace and contentment she had been searching for, paving the way for a more fulfilling and authentic existence.

INTERACTIVE ELEMENT

I would like to invite you to take proactive steps toward managing your stress and improving your well-being. Here's a detailed checklist for readers to identify stress symptoms in their own bodies:

Stress Symptom Checklist

Muscle Tension

- Rate the tension level in your muscles on a scale of 1 to 5 (1 being no tension, 5 being extreme tension).
- Areas to assess: neck, shoulders, jaw, back, arms, and legs.

Headaches

- Rate the frequency and intensity of headaches on a scale of 1 to 5 (1 being rare and mild, 5 being frequent and severe).

- Describe the location and type of headaches (e.g., tension headache, migraine).

Fatigue

- Rate your overall energy levels on a scale of 1 to 5 (1 being high energy, 5 being extreme fatigue).
- Note any patterns of fatigue throughout the day (e.g., morning fatigue, afternoon crashes).

Digestive Issues

- Rate the frequency and severity of digestive symptoms on a scale of 1 to 5 (1 being rare and mild, 5 being frequent and severe).
- Symptoms to assess: stomach pain, nausea, diarrhea, constipation, bloating.

Breathing Difficulty

- Rate the ease of your breathing on a scale of 1 to 5 (1 being easy, 5 being difficult).
- Note any sensations of breathlessness or tightness in the chest.

Heart Rate

- Rate your heart rate or palpitations on a scale of 1 to 5 (1 being normal, 5 being rapid or irregular).
- Pay attention to any noticeable changes in heart rate during rest or activity.

Sleep Disturbances

- Rate the quality and duration of your sleep on a scale of 1 to 5 (1 being restful and sufficient, 5 being restless and inadequate).
- Note any difficulty falling asleep, staying asleep, or waking up feeling refreshed.

Appetite Changes

- Rate any changes in appetite on a scale of 1 to 5 (1 being normal, 5 being significant changes).
- Describe any increase or decrease in appetite, cravings, or disinterest in food.

Skin Conditions

- Rate the presence and severity of any skin issues on a scale of 1 to 5 (1 being clear skin, 5 being severe irritation or breakouts).
- Note any changes in complexion, rashes, itching, or dryness.

Emotional Well-Being

- Rate your overall mood and emotional state on a scale of 1 to 5 (1 being positive and stable, 5 being negative and volatile).
- Describe any feelings of anxiety, irritability, sadness, or overwhelm.

After completing the checklist, review your responses and consider seeking support from a healthcare professional if you notice persistent or severe stress symptoms impacting your daily life.

FINAL THOUGHTS

Concluding this chapter on stress and its intricate ties to the body, it's crucial to reflect on the insights garnered. Throughout our exploration, we've uncovered the profound interplay between stress and physical well-being, looking into various somatic therapy techniques tailored for effective stress management. From addressing the science behind stress, acknowledging its triggers of physiological responses like the fight-or-flight reaction and cortisol release, to discussing self-observation techniques such as mindfulness and body awareness, we've equipped ourselves with tools to identify and address stress symptoms promptly.

Understanding the multifaceted nature of stress, we've recognized its pervasive impact on our lives, affecting not only our physical health but also our emotional and mental well-being. By embracing somatic therapy approaches, we've learned to cultivate resilience and restore balance in the face of stressors, empowering ourselves to navigate life's challenges with greater ease and grace. Through step-by-step instructions in breathwork and other techniques, you now have some valuable tools to work with.

As we move forward, we will get deeper into the realm of somatic therapy, and our focus will shift toward the exploration of trauma and its profound effects on the body. In the upcoming chapter, titled "Healing Trauma through the Body," we'll unravel the intricate layers of trauma, examine how it presents itself physically and emotionally, and explore the transformative potential of somatic therapy in promoting healing and restoration.

CHAPTER THREE

HEALING TRAUMA THROUGH THE BODY

The body remembers trauma long after the mind does; it leaves a mark. It leaves an indelible mark, shaping our physical and emotional well-being, often in ways we might not fully understand. Don't despair, though. This chapter will reveal how our somatic therapy can help release those deeply ingrained memories, making us whole again.

THE LINK BETWEEN EMOTIONAL TRAUMA AND PHYSICAL HEALTH

Trauma is stored in the body in a multitude of ways. This impact may manifest through chronic muscle tension, disruptions in the nervous system, and various other bodily responses. Such trauma is not confined to the realm of the mind; it finds a home within our bodies, affecting our physical and emotional well-being. In this chapter, we will explore the intricate mechanisms by which trauma is trapped in the body and delve into how somatic therapy offers a pathway to release these deeply ingrained memories, ultimately contributing to our overall well-being.

When our brains are subjected to a traumatic event, it can result in a profound impact on our memory systems. As Bessel van der Kolk aptly stated, "Trauma comes back as a reaction, not a memory." This statement highlights a crucial aspect of trauma—it often resurfaces as emotional and physiological reactions rather than neatly organized memories. The reason behind this phenomenon lies in the disruption trauma causes to our declarative explicit memory system, where traumatic memories are not processed and stored in the usual manner. Instead, they can become fragmented, disjointed, and difficult to access consciously. This disruption in memory processing plays a pivotal role in how trauma is experienced and remembered in our bodies and minds.

Understanding "Fight-or-Flight"

Understanding the fight-or-flight response is crucial for understanding how trauma becomes ingrained in the body. This innate physiological reaction is hardwired into our biology and has been essential for our survival throughout human evolution.

When we encounter a threat or a perceived danger, whether physical or emotional, our bodies initiate the fight-or-flight response. This response involves a cascade of physiological changes designed to prepare us for immediate action. The sympathetic nervous system becomes activated, leading to the release of stress hormones like adrenaline and cortisol. These hormones increase heart rate, dilate airways, and redirect blood flow to muscles, effectively priming the body to confront the threat or flee from it.

While this response is conducive to situations such as escaping a predator or responding to a sudden crisis, it can become a real problem in the context of trauma. Individuals who have experienced traumatic events may find themselves stuck in a chronic state of fight-or-flight, even when there is no immediate danger present. This ongoing physiological effect can lead to a range of physical and psychological symptoms, from heightened anxiety and irritability to cardiovascular issues and sleep disturbances.

Traumatic experiences can sensitize the nervous system, making it more prone to react with this heightened response, even to nonthreatening situations. This extended period of heightened physiological activity

can contribute to the development of various somatic symptoms and health problems, underscoring the intricate link between emotional trauma and physical well-being.

A Bit about Cortisol

Healthcare organizations, especially those serving communities with complex needs, often face challenges when engaging their patients, resulting in high no-show rates and noncompliance with recommended treatments. It is crucial to recognize that many individuals and families living in poverty, like those served by the clinic described, are more likely to experience multiple forms of trauma, including physical, emotional, or sexual abuse, neglect, substance use disorders in the family, exposure to violence, and sudden separations from loved ones.

The impact of trauma on health is profound and extends to the physiological level. Traumatic experiences trigger the body's fight, flight, or freeze response, leading to the production of stress hormones such as adrenaline and cortisol. Cortisol, in particular, plays a pivotal role in the body's response to stress, influencing various bodily functions, including metabolism, immune response, and inflammation.

When trauma remains unresolved, it can lead to persistent elevations in cortisol levels, contributing to adverse health outcomes. This prolonged state of physiological arousal can show up in a range of health risk behaviors, including unhealthy eating habits, substance abuse, or risky sexual activities, all of which are associated with chronic diseases and mental health disorders.

To address these challenges, healthcare organizations can adopt a trauma-informed approach, shifting their perspective from asking, "What's wrong with you?" to "What happened to you?" This change in approach fosters empathy and understanding of patients' experiences and behaviors, leading to improved communication and relationship-building. Implementing trauma-informed care, which may include trauma assessment surveys and creating safe, calm environments, not only facilitates patient engagement but also helps regulate cortisol levels and reduce stress-related health risks. Recognizing and addressing the impact of trauma, along with the role of cortisol, is a crucial step toward achieving better healthcare outcomes for vulnerable populations.

SOMATIC EXERCISES FOR TRAUMA

Somatic techniques offer a unique approach to healing that focuses on the mind-body connection. These practices recognize that emotional and psychological experiences are not limited to the mind but are also stored in the body. By exploring somatic techniques, you can begin to address and release stored trauma and stress, ultimately promoting overall well-being. In the following sections, we will delve into various somatic exercises and practices designed to help you reconnect with your body, release tension, and support your healing journey. Below, you will find several categories with exercises, each complete with step-by-step instructions.

Resourcing and Visualization

Creating a Safe Space

Creating and visiting your safe place through this visualization exercise can serve as a valuable resource for finding inner peace and relaxation, especially during challenging times.

Step-by-Step Instructions

Find a Quiet Space: Begin by finding a quiet and comfortable place where you won't be disturbed. Sit or lie down in a relaxed position.

Close Your Eyes: Gently close your eyes to eliminate external distractions and turn your focus inward.

Deep Breathing: Take a few slow, deep breaths. Inhale deeply through your nose, allowing your lungs to fill with air, and then exhale slowly through your mouth. Repeat this several times to relax your body.

Imagine Your Safe Place: Now, start to imagine a place where you feel completely safe and at ease. This could be a real location from your past, a fictional place, or somewhere entirely new. It might be a beach, a forest, a cozy room, or any spot where you feel secure.

Engage Your Senses: As you visualize this safe place, engage all your senses. Imagine what you see, hear, smell, and feel in this environment. Is there a gentle breeze, the sound of ocean waves, or the scent of flowers? Try to make it as vivid as possible.

Explore Details: Take some time to explore the details of your safe place. What colors are predominant? Are there any specific objects or elements that make this place special? The more details you can envision, the more real and comforting it becomes.

Feel the Safety: As you immerse yourself in this visualization, focus on the feeling of safety and calm that it brings you. Let go of any tension or worries, knowing that you can return to this place whenever you need to.

Stay as Long as You Like: Spend as much time as you need in your safe place. You can revisit it in your mind whenever you want to experience its soothing effects.

Gradual Return: When you're ready to end the exercise, slowly bring your awareness back to the present moment. Open your eyes and take a few more deep breaths before resuming your day.

Nature Retreat Visualization

This nature retreat visualization is a powerful way to resource yourself and find solace in times of stress or overwhelm. Regular practice can help you connect with your inner resources and create a mental sanctuary for relaxation and rejuvenation.

Step-by-Step Instructions

Find a Quiet Space: Begin by finding a quiet and comfortable space where you won't be disturbed. Sit in a comfortable position, with your feet flat on the ground and your hands resting on your lap.

Close Your Eyes: Close your eyes gently to block out external distractions. Take a few deep breaths to relax and center yourself.

Imagine a Nature Retreat: Picture in your mind a serene and beautiful natural setting where you feel safe and relaxed. It could be a forest, a beach, a meadow, or any place in nature that resonates with you. Imagine the details of this place, such as the colors, sounds, and scents.

Engage Your Senses: As you visualize your nature retreat, engage your senses:

- **Sight**: Imagine the colors of the landscape, the play of light and shadow, and the beauty of nature around you.
- **Sound:** Listen to the sounds of nature, whether it's the rustling of leaves, the gentle waves of the ocean, or the chirping of birds.
- **Smell:** Imagine the natural scents in the air, whether it's the fragrance of flowers, the freshness of the forest, or the salty sea breeze.
- **Touch:** Feel the textures of the natural elements around you. Run your fingers through the grass, feel the warmth of the sun, or the coolness of a stream.

Explore Your Retreat: In your visualization, start exploring your nature retreat. Walk around, touch the elements, and immerse yourself in the beauty of this place. Notice how peaceful and safe you feel here.

Connect with Your Resources: As you continue to explore, visualize the presence of resources that can support you in times of stress or difficulty. These resources could be represented by symbolic objects or beings in your retreat. For example, you might imagine a wise guide, a healing tree, or a calming stream.

Seek Guidance: If you encounter a symbolic guide in your visualization, you can engage in a brief conversation or seek guidance. Ask your guide for wisdom or support in managing challenges in your life.

Savor the Peace: Spend some time simply savoring the peace and tranquility of your nature retreat. Allow yourself to fully immerse yourself in this safe and nurturing environment.

Return When Ready: When you're ready to conclude the exercise, take a few deep breaths and slowly open your eyes. Carry the sense of peace and resourcefulness from your nature retreat with you into your daily life.

Self-Regulation

Calm Breathing

This calm breathing exercise is a valuable tool for managing emotions and promoting self-regulation. It can be used in moments of stress or anxiety or whenever you need to find a sense of calm and balance in your life. Regular practice can enhance your emotional well-being.

Step-by-Step Instructions

Find a Comfortable Position: Start by finding a comfortable seated or lying down position. You can do this exercise anywhere, but it's helpful to be in a quiet space where you won't be disturbed.

Relax Your Body: Close your eyes gently and take a moment to relax your body. Release any tension you may be holding in your muscles.

Focus on Your Breath: Begin to pay attention to your breath. Take a few natural breaths, noticing the rise and fall of your chest or the expansion and contraction of your abdomen.

Inhale Slowly: Inhale slowly through your nose, counting to four as you breathe in. Feel the air entering your nostrils and filling your lungs. Focus on the sensation of the breath.

Hold Your Breath: At the end of your inhale, hold your breath for a count of two. This pause allows you to center your attention on the breath and prepare for the exhale.

Exhale Slowly: Exhale slowly through your mouth or nose, counting to six as you breathe out. Feel the warm air leaving your body, and pay attention to the sensation of release.

Repeat the Cycle: Continue this pattern of inhaling for four counts, holding for two counts, and exhaling for six counts. You can adjust the counts to a pace that feels comfortable for you.

Focus on the Breath: Keep your attention on your breath throughout the exercise. If your mind starts to wander, gently bring your focus back to the breath.

Visualize Calm: As you continue this rhythmic breathing, you can also visualize a sense of calm and relaxation washing over you with each exhale. Imagine any tension or stress leaving your body with the breath.

Continue for Several Minutes: Practice this controlled breathing exercise for a few minutes or as long as you'd like. It's a portable technique you can use whenever you need to self-regulate and find calmness.

End Mindfully: When you're ready to conclude the exercise, take a few natural breaths and open your eyes. Notice how you feel after this self-regulation practice.

Exercise: Grounding Technique - 5-4-3-2-1

By going through the 5-4-3-2-1 exercise, you bring your attention to the present moment and your immediate surroundings. This can help ground you and reduce feelings of anxiety or dissociation. Practice this technique whenever you need to reconnect with the here and now.

Step-by-Step Instructions

Acknowledge Five Things: Start by identifying and acknowledging five things you can see around you. Look for details in your environment, such as objects, colors, or patterns.

Acknowledge Four Things You Can Touch: Next, focus on four things you can physically touch. Pay attention to the sensations, textures, and temperatures of these objects.

Acknowledge Three Things You Can Hear: Listen for three sounds in your surroundings. They could be natural sounds like birds singing or man-made sounds like a distant car engine.

Acknowledge Two Things You Can Smell: Identify two scents or odors in your vicinity. It could be the smell of a nearby plant, a meal being prepared, or any other fragrance.

Acknowledge One Thing You Can Taste: Finally, consider one thing you can taste, or if that's not possible at the moment, focus on the taste of your own saliva. Be aware of this taste.

Body Scan

Full Body Scan

The body scan exercise allows you to connect with your body and release physical tension, promoting relaxation and self-awareness. Regular practice can help you become more attuned to your body's signals and improve your overall well-being.

Step-by-Step Instructions

Find a Quiet Space: Begin by finding a quiet and comfortable place where you can sit or lie down. Make sure you won't be disturbed during the exercise.

Close Your Eyes: Gently close your eyes to eliminate visual distractions and bring your focus inward.

Deep Breathing: Start with a few deep breaths to relax your body. Inhale slowly through your nose, allowing your abdomen to rise, and exhale slowly through your mouth. Repeat this a few times.

Focus on Your Feet: Direct your attention to your feet. Pay close attention to how they feel. Are they warm or cool? Do you notice any sensations like tingling, pressure, or tension?

Move Upward: Gradually shift your focus to other parts of your body. Move up from your feet to your ankles, calves, knees, thighs, and so on. For each body part, observe any sensations without judgment.

Notice Tension: If you come across areas of tension or discomfort, don't try to change them. Simply observe and acknowledge them. Your awareness alone can promote relaxation.

Continue Upward: Keep moving upward through your body, including your torso, arms, hands, neck, and head. Take your time with each area, and notice any physical sensations you encounter.

Breathe into Tension: If you encounter tension or discomfort, take a slow, deep breath and imagine sending your breath to that area. As you exhale, visualize the tension releasing and melting away.

Whole-Body Awareness: Once you've scanned your entire body, take a moment to sense your body as a whole. Feel the connection between different parts of your body and the ground or surface you're resting on.

Gentle Awakening: When you're ready to end the exercise, start to become aware of your surroundings. Gradually open your eyes and return to the present moment. Take a few more deep breaths before getting up or resuming your activities.

Progressive Muscle Relaxation

Progressive muscle relaxation is a practice that can help you become more aware of physical tension and teach you to let go of it consciously. Regular practice can lead to greater relaxation and reduced muscle tension.

Step-by-Step Instructions

Find a Quiet Space: Sit or lie down in a quiet and comfortable space where you won't be disturbed.

Close Your Eyes: Gently close your eyes to reduce distractions and turn your focus inward.

Take a Deep Breath: Inhale deeply through your nose, allowing your abdomen to rise as you fill your lungs with air.

Start with Your Feet: Begin with your feet. Tense the muscles in your toes and feet as much as you can, and hold this tension for a few seconds.

Release and Relax: After a few seconds, release the tension in your feet completely. Focus on the sensation of relaxation as the tension fades away.

Move Upward: Continue by moving up to your calves and thighs. Tense each muscle group for a few seconds and then release, allowing them to relax.

Check Your Abdomen and Chest: Progress to your abdomen and chest. Tighten these muscle groups briefly and then let go, feeling the relaxation that follows.

Shoulders and Arms: Move on to your shoulders, arms, and hands. Tense and then release each muscle group, one by one.

Neck and Face: Finally, focus on your neck and face. Tense the muscles in your neck, jaw, and facial muscles, and then release them completely.

Take a Deep Breath: Inhale deeply once more, and as you exhale, imagine any remaining tension flowing out of your body.

Stay Relaxed: Remain in this state of relaxation for a few moments, enjoying the sensation of calmness in your body.

Slowly Open Your Eyes: When you're ready, open your eyes and take a moment to transition back to your surroundings.

CASE STUDIES

In our exploration of somatic therapy and its transformative potential, let's delve into real-life case studies that illustrate the remarkable healing journeys of individuals who have harnessed the power of somatic practices to overcome trauma and restore their well-being. These stories offer valuable insights into the profound impact of somatic therapy on the lives of those who have embarked on this path to healing.

Rachel's Journey

Rachel, a thirty-four-year-old marketer, had just received a long-awaited promotion to CEO of Marketing at her firm. She had been striving for advancement, but upon learning it entailed public speaking presentations to clients, she panicked. She was faced with the choice of giving up her dream job or confronting her fears. She chose to tackle her issues head-on.

One day, while searching for ways to cope with her overwhelming fear of public speaking, Rachel stumbled upon somatic therapy and its exercises for healing. She decided to give it a try with the help of a therapist, starting with the resourcing and visualization exercise.

Rachel learned that, unknowingly, she had been carrying the weight of past traumas for years. She struggled with anxiety, sleepless nights, and a constant feeling of unease. The burden of her traumatic experiences, including a childhood accident and an abusive relationship, had taken a toll on her physical and emotional well-being.

As she learned and practiced resourcing, Rachel created a mental sanctuary, a safe haven where she could escape when anxiety threatened to overwhelm her. She visualized a tranquil beach, feeling the warmth of the sand beneath her feet and the gentle breeze against her skin. This exercise provided her with a sense of security and comfort she hadn't felt in years.

Rachel also embraced the self-regulation exercise, which helped her regain control over her emotions. By practicing self-regulation techniques, she learned to recognize when her body was reacting to past traumas and could take steps to calm herself down. This newfound skill allowed her to navigate challenging situations like client presentations with greater ease, and she excelled in her new position. Her journey to healing serves as a testament to the power of somatic techniques in overcoming the lasting effects of trauma and reclaiming one's life.

Alex's Awakening

Alex, a thirty-five-year-old software engineer in California, had been struggling with commitment issues in his romantic relationships for years. His journey toward healing began when he discovered somatic therapy and decided to give it a try.

Alex's therapist introduced him to a grounding and resourcing exercise that aimed to help him manage his fear of commitment and emotional vulnerability. Through mindful breathing, body awareness techniques, and visualization, Alex learned to stay present in his relationships without feeling overwhelmed by anxiety. Additionally, he practiced the mindful movement exercise to release tension and connect with his body.

As Alex continued his somatic therapy sessions, he noticed a significant improvement in his ability to connect with his partner and address his commitment fears. The combination of grounding and resourcing, along with mindful movement, had equipped him with essential skills to navigate his emotions and build healthier, more fulfilling relationships. Alex's story highlights the transformative potential of somatic therapy, empowering individuals like him to overcome their emotional barriers and find deeper connection and intimacy.

Stacy

Meet Stacy, a twenty-eight-year-old mother of two who had been carrying the weight of generational trauma for as long as she could remember. Growing up in a household marked by substance abuse and emotional neglect, Stacy knew she wanted to break the cycle and provide a healthier environment for her own children.

One day, while seeking guidance and support, Stacy discovered somatic therapy. Determined to heal and end the generational trauma, she embarked on a journey of self-discovery and transformation. Her therapist introduced her to a unique exercise called "Emotional Release through Movement."

This exercise encouraged Stacy to express her emotions physically, using movement and dance as a form of catharsis. Through the rhythmic flow of her body, Stacy was able to release pent-up emotions, confront past traumas, and regain a sense of empowerment. As she danced, she imagined shedding the generational burdens that had plagued her family for years.

Stacy found herself more attuned to her emotions and better equipped to handle life's challenges. She noticed positive changes not only within herself but also in her interactions with her children. By embracing somatic therapy and the transformative power of movement, Stacy had taken a significant step toward breaking the cycle of generational trauma and creating a brighter, healthier future for her family.

INTERACTIVE ELEMENT

Next, you'll discover an interactive element within the pages of this book, empowering you to embark on a journey of trauma release, offering you a pathway to healing and transformation.

20-Minute Trauma Release Exercise

This exercise is a tool for self-care and healing. You can practice it regularly to gradually release stored tension and trauma from your body, promoting a greater sense of well-being.

Find Your Space: Choose a quiet and comfortable space where you won't be disturbed. Ensure the room is well-ventilated.

Comfortable Seating or Lying Down: Sit or lie down in a comfortable position. You can use a yoga mat or lie directly on a carpeted floor or bed.

Begin Deep Breathing: Close your eyes and take a few deep breaths. Inhale through your nose for a count of four, hold for a count of four, and exhale through your mouth for a count of four. Repeat this pattern for a few minutes to calm your mind.

Scan Body: Start at the top of your head and slowly scan your body mentally. Notice any areas of tension, discomfort, or tightness. Pay attention to any sensations or emotions that arise.

Progressive Muscle Relaxation: Begin with your toes and work your way up through your body. Tense each muscle group for a few seconds, then release. Focus on the contrast between tension and relaxation.

Mindful Movement: Gently introduce movement to your body. You can start with slow, mindful stretches or yoga poses. Move in a way that feels comfortable for you, paying attention to your breath and sensations.

Release Tension: As you move, visualize tension and stress leaving your body with each exhalation. Imagine these negative energies dissolving into the air around you.

Guided Imagery (Optional): If you feel comfortable, incorporate guided imagery. Imagine a peaceful and safe place where you can let go of any remaining stress or trauma. Visualize yourself becoming lighter and freer.

Breathing and Grounding: Return to deep breathing for a few minutes, focusing on the present moment. Feel the connection between your body and the ground beneath you.

Closing Reflection: Slowly transition back to a seated position. Take a moment to reflect on how you feel after the exercise. Notice any positive changes in your body and mind. End the exercise with an open heart, carrying the sense of release and peace with you into your day.

FINAL THOUGHTS

You learned about the powerful connection between emotional trauma and your physical well-being. This chapter explored how trauma can be stored in your body, leading to long-lasting effects on both your emotional and physical health.

We discussed the fight-or-flight response, which, while essential for survival, can become problematic when dealing with trauma. Trauma can sensitize your nervous system, causing extended periods of heightened physical reactions and potentially leading to various health issues.

The role of cortisol, a stress hormone, in the body's response to trauma was explained, highlighting the importance of recognizing and addressing its impact on your health, especially if you're part of a vulnerable population.

You were introduced to somatic exercises designed to help release trauma from your body. These exercises, categorized as *resourcing, visualization*, and *self-regulation*, were explained in detail, with step-by-step instructions to follow.

As you move forward, remember to put into practice what you've learned in this chapter. Recognize the profound impact that somatic therapy can have on releasing trauma from your body and improving your overall well-being. In the next chapter, we'll explore how to establish a harmonious relationship between your mental and physical selves, a crucial step in your journey toward holistic healing and wellness.

CHAPTER FOUR

BRIDGING MIND AND BODY

I magine your body as a library; each muscle and fiber is a shelf filled with stories. Some stories are joyful, while others are marked by pain and suffering. In this chapter, we will explore how your body becomes the keeper of these tales and how understanding this library of experiences can lead to profound healing. Are you ready to unlock the secrets of your own story hidden within the very fibers of your being?

DEVELOPING MIND-BODY CONNECTION STRATEGIES

Paula, a thirty-three-year-old woman, was constantly stressed with reoccurring thoughts of the past. She had lost her husband and baby in a car crash. Although it had been eight years, and she had spent most of those years in talk therapy counseling, she felt stuck. It was as if the wreck had happened yesterday. Paula suffered from horrible migraines, and the weight of her grief bore down on her every day.

One day, while browsing a local bookstore, Paula stumbled across a book on mindfulness. Intrigued, she began to read and decided to try the exercises within. As she practiced mindfulness, Paula started to notice the tension she held in her neck and shoulders—a physical manifestation of her unprocessed grief.

By repeating these mindfulness exercises day after day and becoming more and more aware of the connection between her mind and body, Paula began to feel a gradual but profound relief. The migraines that had plagued her for years became less frequent, and the heavy burden of her past began to lighten.

Paula's journey of healing had begun in the quiet moments of self-awareness, and it would lead her to discover the transformative power of her own body in releasing trauma. These techniques, like mindfulness and guided imagery, which have already been introduced, can do the same for you as well.

Mindful Breathing

One of the first things clients learn in somatic-based therapy is the art of mindful breathing. While it may seem elementary, it is extremely important in trauma therapy and also provides a firm foundation for further work. Mindful breathing is a simple yet powerful technique that involves focusing your attention on your breath. You don't need any special equipment or a specific location; you can practice it anywhere, at any time. The beauty of mindful breathing lies in its accessibility. It's a tool you carry with you, always at your disposal, ready to bring you back to the present moment and help you establish a stronger connection between your mind and body.

The way it works is that by directing your awareness to the rhythmic flow of your breath, you create a bridge between your thoughts and your physical self. This simple act of attention redirects your focus away from racing thoughts or distressing memories, grounding you in the present. As you inhale and exhale deliberately, you become attuned to subtle bodily sensations, enabling you to identify and release tension, ultimately fostering a deeper mind-body connection.

Mindful Exercise

As previously discussed, mindful breathing is a fundamental yet potent form of mindfulness meditation. It involves directing your awareness to your breath—the natural cadence of your inhales and exhales, as well as the sensory experience associated with each breath. Here is a simple exercise you can do almost anywhere, anytime:

Mindful Breathing Meditation

Step-by-Step Instructions: Lighthouse Meditation: Guiding Your Inner Light

Step 1: Find a Quiet Space

Begin by finding a quiet and comfortable space where you won't be disturbed. Sit or lie down in a relaxed position.

Step 2: Close Your Eyes

Gently close your eyes to eliminate external distractions and turn your focus inward.

Step 3: Deep Breathing

Take a few slow, deep breaths. Inhale deeply through your nose, allowing your lungs to fill with air, and then exhale slowly through your mouth. Repeat this several times to relax your body.

Step 4: Visualization – The Lighthouse

Visualize yourself standing on a serene, rocky coastline. In front of you stands a majestic lighthouse. This lighthouse represents your inner strength, wisdom, and clarity.

Step 5: Guiding Light

Imagine yourself climbing the spiral staircase inside the lighthouse. As you ascend, each step brings you closer to your inner light.

Step 6: Inner Sanctuary

At the top of the lighthouse, you reach a small balcony with a breathtaking view of the ocean. This balcony is your inner sanctuary, a place of peace and serenity.

Step 7: Illuminate Your Mind

As you stand on the balcony, imagine a brilliant light at the center of your being. This light represents your inner wisdom and clarity. Visualize it growing brighter with each breath you take.

Step 8: Let It Shine

Imagine this inner light expanding beyond your body, filling the entire lighthouse with its radiant glow. Feel it radiating warmth, love, and guidance.

Step 9: Connect with Your True Self

As the lighthouse illuminates the coastline, imagine it also illuminating your mind and spirit. Feel a deep sense of connection with your true self, free from distractions and doubts.

Step 10: Reflect and Absorb

Take a moment to reflect on any questions or challenges you may have in your life. Allow the inner light to provide insights and answers.

Step 11: Gratitude

Express gratitude for this moment of clarity and connection with your inner wisdom.

Step 12: Return When Ready

When you're ready to end the meditation, slowly descend the staircase inside the lighthouse. As you descend, know that you can return to this inner sanctuary whenever you seek guidance and clarity.

Step 13: Open Your Eyes

Open your eyes, feeling refreshed and grounded, carrying the wisdom and clarity of your inner light with you into your day.

Mindful Breathing Can Change Your Day (and Your Life)

Mindful breathing is a simple yet transformative practice that can significantly impact your well-being, both in the short and long term. By incorporating mindful breathing into your daily routine, you can experience a range of benefits that can change the course of your day and even your life.

Mindful Breathing Benefits

- **Pain Relief**: Mindful breathing has been linked to pain relief, helping individuals manage discomfort more effectively.
- **Stress Reduction**: One of its most renowned benefits, mindful breathing can rapidly reduce stress levels, promoting a sense of calm and relaxation.
- **Anxiety Reduction**: Mindful breathing is a powerful tool in managing anxiety, providing a sense of control over racing thoughts and worries.
- **Reduced Cravings**: Whether it's sugar, alcohol, cigarettes, or anything else you are trying to quit, mindful breathing can help.
- **Less Negative Thinking:** It helps reduce negative thinking patterns and negative self-talk, fostering a more positive mindset.
- **Increased Compassion:** Regular practice can lead to increased compassion toward oneself and others, enhancing relationships and empathy.
- **Improved Cognitive Functions:** Mindful breathing positively impacts memory, attention, and focus, aiding in better decision-making and productivity.
- **Improved Sleep**: It can contribute to improved sleep quality, helping those with insomnia or sleep disturbances.
- **Improved Brain Health**: Studies suggest that mindful breathing can lead to structural changes in the brain associated with improved emotional regulation and overall well-being.

Why Does Mindful Breathing Work?

Mindful breathing works by engaging the body's relaxation response, reducing the production of stress hormones, and promoting a state of calmness. It also increases self-awareness, allowing individuals to recognize and manage their emotional responses more effectively.

Types of Meditation Breathing Techniques

There are various meditation breathing techniques, including diaphragmatic breathing, box breathing, 2-4 breathing, and 4-7-8 breathing, each with its own unique approach to achieving relaxation and mindfulness. These techniques provide individuals with the flexibility to choose the one that best suits their needs and preferences.

Incorporating mindful breathing into your daily life can be a profound step toward achieving emotional balance, mental clarity, and overall well-being. It's a simple practice with the potential to bring about significant positive changes, making it a valuable tool for improving your day-to-day life and long-term health.

Step-by-Step Instructions for 2-4 Breathing Exercises

Step 1: Find a Comfortable Position

Sit in a comfortable chair or lie down on your back in a quiet and relaxed environment. Close your eyes if it feels comfortable to do so.

Step 2: Focus on Your Breath

Take a moment to bring your awareness to your breath.

Notice the natural rhythm of your breathing without trying to change it.

Step 3: Inhale Slowly

Begin by inhaling deeply through your nose. As you inhale, count silently to yourself for a count of two.

Step 4: Hold Your Breath

After you have fully inhaled, hold your breath for a count of four seconds.

Maintain a comfortable level of breath retention without straining.

Step 5: Exhale Slowly

Release your breath slowly and steadily through your mouth.

Exhale for a count of four seconds, allowing your breath to naturally leave your body.

Step 6: Repeat the Cycle

Continue the pattern of inhaling for two counts, holding for four counts, and exhaling for four counts. Aim to maintain a smooth and steady rhythm throughout the exercise.

Step 7: Focus on Relaxation

As you continue the breathing exercise, focus on relaxing your body and mind with each breath cycle. Let go of any tension or stress with each exhale, allowing yourself to sink deeper into relaxation.

Step 8: Practice for Several Minutes

Repeat the 2-4 breathing exercise for several minutes, gradually extending the duration if desired. Start with a few minutes and gradually increase to five or ten minutes as you become more comfortable with the practice.

Step 9: Be Mindful of Your Body

Pay attention to how your body feels as you engage in the breathing exercise. Notice any sensations of relaxation, calmness, or clarity that arise with each breath cycle.

Step 10: Conclude Mindfully

When you're ready to conclude the exercise, take a few final deep breaths and gently open your eyes if they were closed.

Take a moment to acknowledge the benefits of the practice and carry the sense of relaxation and calmness with you into your day.

Emotional Regulation

Emotional regulation refers to the ability to manage and control your emotions effectively. Developing these skills can help individuals navigate the complexities of their emotional landscapes with greater ease, fostering resilience, enhancing interpersonal relationships, and contributing to overall mental and physical well-being:

Step-by-Step Instructions for Emotional Regulation

Step 1: Recognize and Identify Emotions

- Take a moment to pause and identify what you're feeling.
- Name the emotion you're experiencing (e.g., anger, sadness, anxiety).

Step 2: Understand Triggers

- Reflect on what triggers your emotions.
- Identify specific situations, thoughts, or interactions that tend to evoke strong emotional responses.

Step 3: Practice Mindfulness

- Practice mindfulness techniques such as deep breathing, meditation, or body scanning to bring awareness to your present-moment experience.
- Notice physical sensations, thoughts, and emotions without judgment.

Step 4: Develop Coping Strategies

Identify healthy coping mechanisms that help you manage difficult emotions. Experiment with strategies such as deep breathing exercises, progressive muscle relaxation, journaling, or talking to a trusted friend or therapist.

Step 5: Reframe Negative Thoughts

Challenge and reframe negative or unhelpful thoughts that contribute to intense emotions. Replace irrational or distorted thoughts with more realistic and balanced perspectives.

Step 6: Express Emotions Constructively

- Find healthy ways to express and communicate your emotions.
- Practice assertive communication techniques to express your needs and boundaries effectively.

Step 7: Set Boundaries

- Establish boundaries to protect your emotional well-being.
- Learn to say no when necessary and prioritize self-care.

Step 8: Seek Support

Reach out to supportive friends, family members, or mental health professionals for guidance and encouragement. Consider therapy or counseling to explore underlying issues and learn additional coping skills.

Step 9: Practice Self-Compassion

Be kind and compassionate toward yourself, especially during challenging times. Remember that it's okay to experience a range of emotions, and you're not alone in your struggles.

Step 10: Reflect and Evaluate

Regularly reflect on your emotional experiences and the effectiveness of your coping strategies. Adjust and refine your approach based on what works best for you over time.

Guided Imagery

Guided imagery is a powerful relaxation technique that involves using your imagination to create sensory-rich experiences in your mind. It is a purposeful and systematic practice where you imagine yourself in a peaceful and calming environment or situation. The goal is to engage your senses and immerse yourself fully in the mental experience, thereby promoting relaxation, reducing stress, and enhancing emotional management.

Effectiveness in Stress Reduction and Emotional Management

Guided imagery is highly effective in stress reduction and emotional management because it taps into the mind's ability to influence the body. By visualizing serene and positive scenarios, individuals can trigger the relaxation response, which counteracts the stress response. This, in turn, leads to a decrease in stress hormones, a lowered heart rate, and an overall sense of calm. Guided imagery can also help individuals gain a sense of control over their emotions, reduce anxiety, and improve mood.

Here are a few vivid guided imagery scenarios for you to try:

- **Beach Escape**: Imagine yourself standing on a pristine, sun-kissed beach. Feel the warm sand beneath your toes, listen to the gentle lapping of waves, and smell the salt in the air. Visualize the vibrant colors of the ocean and the sky. As you soak in the tranquility of the beach, let go of any stress or tension.
- **Forest Retreat**: Picture yourself in a lush forest. Hear the rustling of leaves, the chirping of birds, and the babbling of a clear stream. Feel the coolness of the forest floor beneath your feet. Allow the sights and sounds of nature to envelop you, filling you with peace and serenity.

- **Mountain Serenity**: Visualize standing on the summit of a majestic mountain. Experience the crisp mountain air, the panoramic views, and the sense of accomplishment. As you gaze at the vast expanse before you, feel a deep sense of calm and inner strength.
- **Floating on Clouds**: Envision yourself lying on a soft, fluffy cloud high in the sky. Feel the cloud's gentle support beneath you as you float weightlessly. Look down at the world below and let go of any worries or stress, knowing that you are safe and at peace.
- **Candlelit Oasis:** Picture yourself in a tranquil oasis illuminated by candlelight. Hear the soothing crackle of candles and the distant trickle of a fountain. Feel the softness of cushions beneath you as you relax in this serene space. Allow the ambiance to wash away tension and promote inner calm.

These guided imagery scenarios can be customized so you can do them anytime, anywhere. You can also tailor them to your likes and dislikes.

Guided Imagery Techniques

Different guided imagery techniques can help you achieve different goals. Some of the most popular techniques include:

- **Imagining a Peaceful Scene**: This technique involves envisioning yourself in a tranquil and calming environment to soothe anxiety or relieve stress. You can create a mental image of a place where you feel safe and at ease, such as a beach, forest, or meadow. Focus on sensory details like the sights, sounds, and sensations of this peaceful location. As you immerse yourself in this mental retreat, let go of tension and allow a sense of calm to wash over you.

- **Visualizing White Blood Cells:** In this technique, you can harness the power of your imagination to visualize white blood cells actively fighting illness, whether it's an infection or cancer. Picture these microscopic defenders as courageous warriors, bravely attacking and eliminating any harmful invaders within your body. This imagery can boost your immune system and provide a sense of empowerment in your battle against illness.
- **Imagining a Successful Outcome**: Visualization can be a potent tool for achieving success in various aspects of life. Whether you're preparing for an athletic event, striving to quit smoking, or facing any challenge, you can use guided imagery to imagine a successful outcome. Visualize yourself performing at your best, overcoming obstacles, and achieving your goals. This mental rehearsal can enhance your confidence and motivation, increasing the likelihood of a positive outcome.

Guided imagery techniques allow you to tap into the creative power of your mind to promote relaxation, improve well-being, and work toward personal growth and success. By harnessing the vivid imagery of your imagination, you can positively influence your emotions, behaviors, and overall mental and physical health.

Step-by-Step Guided Imagery Meditation Exercises

These guided imagery exercises can help you manage stress, enhance well-being, and achieve your goals through the power of visualization.

Exercise 1: Imagining a Peaceful Scene

Step 1: Find a Quiet Place

Begin by locating a quiet and comfortable place where you won't be interrupted. Sit or lie down in a relaxed position.

Step 2: Close Your Eyes

Gently close your eyes to block out external distractions and shift your focus inward.

Step 3: Deep Breathing

Take a few slow, deep breaths to relax your body. Inhale deeply through your nose, allowing your lungs to fill with air, and then exhale slowly through your mouth. Repeat this several times to calm your mind.

Step 4: Choose Your Peaceful Place

Start to imagine a place where you feel completely safe and at ease. This could be a real location from your past, a fictional place, or somewhere entirely new. It might be one of the scenes above or any other spot where you feel secure.

Step 5: Engage Your Senses

As you visualize this safe place, engage all your senses. Imagine what you see, hear, smell, and feel in this environment. Picture the details vividly—whether it's the gentle breeze, the sound of ocean waves, or the scent of flowers.

Step 6: Explore Details

Take some time to explore the details of your safe place. Observe the predominant colors, specific objects or elements that make this place special, and any unique features that stand out.

Step 7: Feel the Safety

As you immerse yourself in this visualization, focus on the feeling of safety and calm that it brings you. Let go of any tension or worries, knowing that you can return to this place whenever you need to.

Step 8: Stay as Long as You Like

Spend as much time as you need in your safe place. You can revisit it in your mind whenever you want to experience its soothing effects.

Step 9: Gradual Return

When you're ready to end the exercise, slowly bring your awareness back to the present moment. Open your eyes and take a few more deep breaths before resuming your day.

Exercise 2: Visualizing White Blood Cells

Step 1: Prepare in a Quiet Space

Find a quiet and comfortable place to sit or lie down where you can focus without distractions.

Step 2: Close Your Eyes

Close your eyes gently and take a few deep breaths to relax and center yourself.

Step 3: Picture Your Body

Visualize your own body from within. Imagine yourself at a microscopic level, focusing on the area where you want to promote healing and wellness.

Step 4: Visualize White Blood Cells

Begin to visualize white blood cells within your body. See them as powerful, determined warriors dressed in bright amor.

Step 5: The Battle Begins

Envision these white blood cells actively patrolling your body, seeking out and targeting any harmful invaders like infections or cancer cells. Picture them engaging in battle, surrounding and eliminating the threats.

Step 6: Strength and Victory

Imagine these white blood cells as strong, relentless defenders. See them triumphing over illness and restoring your body's health.

Step 7: Feel Empowered

As you visualize this process, feel a sense of empowerment and confidence in your body's ability to heal and protect itself.

Step 8: Stay in This Visualization

Remain in this visualization for as long as you like, letting the imagery fill you with a sense of well-being and strength.

Step 9: Gradual Return

When you're ready to conclude, take a few deep breaths and slowly open your eyes. Carry this feeling of empowerment and healing with you into your day.

Exercise 3: Imagining a Successful Outcome

Step 1: Create a Quiet Space

Find a quiet and comfortable place to sit or lie down where you can fully focus on your visualization.

Step 2: Close Your Eyes

Close your eyes gently and take a few deep breaths to calm your mind.

Step 3: Define Your Goal

Clearly define the goal or challenge you want to address through this exercise. It could be related to sports, quitting smoking, or any personal aspiration.

Step 4: Visualize Success

Begin to visualize a scenario where you have already achieved your goal successfully. See yourself in action, performing at your best, and reaching the desired outcome.

Step 5: Engage Your Senses

As you visualize, engage all your senses. Imagine what you see, hear, feel, and even taste in this successful moment. Make it as vivid as possible.

Step 6: Embrace Positive Emotions

Feel the positive emotions associated with this success. Experience the joy, satisfaction, and confidence that come with achieving your goal.

Step 7: Overcome Challenges

If you encounter challenges or obstacles in your visualization, see yourself overcoming them with determination and resilience.

Step 8: Repetition and Reinforcement

Repeat this visualization regularly, reinforcing the image of your successful outcome. This mental rehearsal can boost your motivation and self-belief.

Step 9: Gradual Return

When you're ready to end the exercise, take a few deep breaths and slowly open your eyes. Carry the confidence and determination from your visualization into your actions and decisions.

Guided Imagery Tips

Guided imagery is a personal practice, and there is no right or wrong way to do it. It's about finding what works best for you and incorporating it into your self-care routine to promote relaxation, reduce stress, and achieve your goals.

Choose a Quiet and Comfortable Space: Find a peaceful and distraction-free environment where you can comfortably sit or lie down. Dim the lights if it helps create a more relaxed atmosphere.

Deep Breathing: Before starting guided imagery, take a few deep breaths to relax your body and clear your mind. Deep breathing helps you transition into a calm state.

Set Clear Intentions: Know the purpose of your guided imagery session. Whether it's for relaxation, stress reduction, or achieving a specific goal, having a clear intention will guide your visualization.

Visualize Vividly: Engage all your senses when visualizing. Imagine the sights, sounds, smells, textures, and even tastes associated with the scenario you're visualizing. The more vivid, the better.

Emotions Matter: Pay attention to the emotions you experience during the imagery. Positive emotions enhance the effectiveness of the exercise. Feel the joy, peace, confidence, and gratitude in your visualization.

Practice Regularly: Consistency is key. The more you practice guided imagery, the more effective it becomes. Consider incorporating it into your daily routine for lasting benefits.

Keep It Positive: Focus on positive and empowering imagery. Avoid negative or distressing scenarios, as they can create unwanted emotions and stress.

Use Guided Recordings: Guided imagery recordings led by experienced practitioners can be helpful, especially if you're new to the practice. You can find a variety of guided imagery sessions online or through apps.

Customize Your Imagery: Tailor the imagery to your specific needs. If you're using it for stress reduction, create scenarios that bring you peace and calm. To achieve goals, visualize successful outcomes.

Trust the Process: Be patient with yourself. Guided imagery may take some time to show noticeable effects, so trust the process and allow the benefits to accumulate over time.

Combine with Other Techniques: Guided imagery can complement other relaxation techniques, such as deep breathing, mindfulness, or progressive muscle relaxation, for a more comprehensive approach to well-being.

Reflect Afterward: Take a moment after each session to reflect on your experience. Journaling your thoughts, feelings, and any insights gained can help you track progress and identify patterns.

Seek Professional Guidance: If you have specific mental health concerns or trauma, consider consulting a mental health professional who can guide you in using guided imagery effectively and safely.

Guided Imagery at Home

Many people practice guided imagery during individual somatic therapy sessions, and others engage in group sessions. But did you know you can do guided imagery by yourself in your own home? This can be accomplished using Guided Imagery Scripts for Neurofeedback Home Therapy. These are specific scripts designed to facilitate guided imagery exercises as part of neurofeedback therapy. The scripts are meticulously crafted narratives or sets of instructions that help individuals visualize and immerse themselves in mental images that promote relaxation, healing, and the achievement of therapeutic goals. The scripts can vary widely, targeting different issues or goals, such as reducing anxiety, enhancing sleep quality, improving concentration, or fostering a deeper connection with one's body and emotions.To engage in Guided Imagery Scripts for Neurofeedback Home Therapy, follow these steps:

Step 1: Set the Scene

Find a quiet and comfortable space in your home where you won't be disturbed.

Step 2: Choose a Script

Select a guided imagery script that aligns with your therapeutic goals.

Relaxation: Begin by taking deep breaths and calming your mind.

Visualization: Read or listen to the script, immersing yourself in the imagery and sensory details.

Emotional Engagement: Feel the emotions associated with the scenario deeply.

Consistency: Practice regularly to reinforce desired neural pathways and optimize neurofeedback outcomes.

By following these steps, you can harness the power of guided imagery scripts for neurofeedback therapy in the comfort of your home, promoting mental well-being and positive neurological changes.

The Importance of Body Awareness

Body awareness is a fundamental aspect of holistic well-being. It involves tuning into physical sensations, emotions, and the mind-body connection. Recognizing bodily signals can aid in stress reduction, emotional regulation, and early detection of discomfort or tension. This heightened awareness fosters a deeper understanding of one's physical and emotional needs, empowering individuals to make healthier choices and manage stress effectively. Embracing body awareness contributes to a more balanced and harmonious life.

Benefits of Body Awareness

Body awareness offers a range of benefits, including:

- **Better Balance and Stability**: Being in tune with your body helps improve balance and stability, reducing the risk of falls and injuries.

- **Weight Management:** By recognizing hunger and fullness cues, you can better manage your eating habits, contributing to weight control.
- **Pain Management:** Increased awareness allows you to identify and address physical discomfort more effectively, potentially reducing chronic pain.
- **Identifying and Meeting Your Needs**: Understanding your body's signals enables you to meet its needs, whether it's rest, hydration, or nourishment.
- **Improved Mental and Emotional Well-being**: Research studies have indicated that cultivating body awareness through practices such as mindfulness, yoga, or body scan exercises has been associated with improvements in emotional regulation and overall well-being. For example, a study published in the Journal of Psychosomatic Research found that individuals who regularly engaged in mindfulness practices showed increased emotional regulation skills and reported greater subjective well-being compared to those who did not engage in such practices (Brown & Ryan, 2003).

Body Awareness Real-Life Success Stories

James' Story

James Anderson struggled with chronic back pain due to a sedentary lifestyle. Determined to find a solution, he turned to yoga and mindfulness. With consistent practice, he regained flexibility and strength and reduced his pain. This transformation improved not only his physical health but also his mental and emotional well-being, bringing him a renewed sense of vitality and peace.

Emily's Story

Emily Thompson's weight loss journey was uniquely guided by a combination of cognitive behavioral therapy (CBT) and somatic therapy. Struggling with excess weight and its emotional toll, Emily turned to these therapies for help. Through CBT, she addressed emotional eating patterns and tackled underlying issues. Simultaneously, somatic therapy enhanced her mind-body connection.

Emily's progress was remarkable. As the pounds melted away, so did her negative self-image, resulting in a more confident and mentally healthier version of herself. Emily's story highlights the transformative potential of holistic therapies, demonstrating that weight loss can be more than just physical—it can be deeply emotional and psychological.

Kelly's Story

Kelly's journey to recovery from addiction was marked by her determination and the support of guided therapy. Struggling with addiction for years, she turned to guided therapy as a complementary approach to traditional treatment. Through guided therapy, she developed coping strategies, gained insight into her triggers, and found the strength to overcome addiction, ultimately reclaiming her life.

Enhancing Body Awareness and Mindfulness

Body awareness is the practice of tuning into the physical sensations, movements, and feedback from your body. It involves consciously directing your attention to different parts of your body to gain a deeper understanding of your physical and emotional state. This process typically involves the following steps:

- **Focus**: Start by choosing a specific area or aspect of your body to focus on. It could be your breath, a particular muscle group, or a physical sensation.
- **Observation**: Once you've chosen a focus, observe it without judgment. Pay attention to any sensations, tension, or discomfort in that area.
- **Breath Awareness:** Often, body awareness is combined with mindful breathing. Sync your breath with your focus area, using your breath as a tool to explore and release tension.
- **Acceptance:** Practice acceptance of whatever you discover during your body awareness exercise. Avoid judgment or criticism, and instead, acknowledge your sensations and emotions.
- **Emotional Connection**: Recognize the link between physical sensations and emotions. Understand how stress, anxiety, or other emotions manifest in your body.
- **Regular Practice**: Developing body awareness is an ongoing practice. Consistency is key to deepening your connection with your body and understanding its signals.
- **Integration:** Over time, integrate body awareness into your daily life. Use it to manage stress, make healthier choices, and improve your overall well-being.

Body awareness fosters a stronger mind-body connection, helping individuals become more attuned to their physical and emotional needs. It can be a powerful tool for promoting self-regulation, relaxation, and holistic well-being.

Introduction to Daily Practices

Start by introducing simple daily practices to enhance body awareness. One effective technique is mindful walking, where you focus your attention on each step, your body's movements, and the sensations in your feet as they touch the ground.

Benefits in Everyday Life

Emphasize the numerous benefits of these practices in daily life. Increased body awareness can lead to better self-regulation, reduced stress, improved posture, and heightened overall mindfulness. These practices empower individuals to stay present and attuned to their bodies, fostering a deeper connection between the mind and body.

Body Awareness and Sensory Processes

These sensory processes are essential for body awareness, movement control, and overall coordination. They allow you to interact effectively with your environment, perform tasks, and navigate through daily life.

- **Proprioception**: Proprioception is your body's ability to sense its position, movements, and actions. It involves receptors in your muscles, tendons, and joints that provide feedback to your brain about the relative position of body parts. This information helps you coordinate movements and maintain balance.
- **Kinesthesia:** Kinesthesia, often referred to as the sixth sense, is closely related to proprioception. It involves perceiving the motion of your body parts and their relative positions in real time. This sense allows you to perform precise movements, such as catching a ball or typing on a keyboard.

- **Visual & Vestibular Systems:** The visual system relies on visual cues to perceive the environment and orient yourself. The vestibular system, located in your inner ear, provides information about your head's position and movement. These two systems work together to help you maintain balance and spatial awareness.
- **Sensory Integration**: Sensory integration is the process of the brain combining information from various sensory systems (e.g., touch, sight, hearing) to create a coherent perception of the world. It enables you to make sense of your surroundings and respond appropriately to sensory input.

Body Awareness Exercises

Here are step-by-step instructions for enhancing body awareness and mindfulness through practices related to proprioception, kinesthesia, the visual and vestibular systems, and sensory integration:

Proprioception and Kinesthesia

Body Scan: Start by finding a quiet space to sit or lie down. Close your eyes and take a few deep breaths to relax.

Focus on Body Parts: Begin by bringing your attention to specific body parts, such as your feet. Without looking, try to sense the position and movement of your feet. Are they relaxed or tense? Are they still or in motion?

Progressive Scan: Gradually move your attention up through your body, paying close attention to each part. Notice any sensations or tensions. Try to sense the position of your limbs and their relationship to each other.

Mindful Movements: Stand up and perform slow, deliberate movements like raising your arms or walking. Pay full attention to the sensations and positions of your body as you move.

Visual & Vestibular Systems

Eye Movements: Sit comfortably and focus on an object in the room. Slowly move your gaze to different objects without turning your head. Notice how your eyes adjust to the changes in focus.

Head Movements: While sitting, gently turn your head from side to side and up and down. Pay attention to how your vestibular system helps you maintain balance and a sense of orientation.

Sensory Integration

Sensory Exploration: Engage in sensory activities like touching different textures, listening to various sounds, and even tasting different foods mindfully. Combine multiple sensory experiences to see how they interact.

Mindful Observation: Find a natural scene outdoors or an interesting object indoors. Observe it closely, using all your senses. What do you see, hear, smell, and possibly even taste or touch?

Body Awareness for Beginners

By incorporating these practices into your daily life, you can gradually enhance your body awareness and mindfulness, leading to a deeper connection with your physical self.

Visual Observation: Start by examining anatomical illustrations or photographs of the human body. Pay attention to the different parts, organs, and structures. This visual exploration helps you familiarize yourself with the body's complexity.

Balance Exercises: Incorporate balance exercises into your routine. Stand on one foot while maintaining stability, and then switch to the other. This engages proprioception, which is your sense of body position and movement.

Sense of Symmetry: Develop an awareness of symmetry in your body. Notice how each side feels and moves. Are there any differences or imbalances between your left and right sides? This practice promotes kinesthesia, which is the awareness of body movement.

Breath Awareness: Pay close attention to your breath. Feel the rise and fall of your chest and abdomen as you breathe. This fosters sensory integration by connecting your breath with bodily sensations.

Mindful Walking: Practice mindful walking by taking slow, deliberate steps and focusing on each sensation as your foot touches the ground. This helps you integrate visual, proprioceptive, and kinesthetic cues.

Body Scanning: Dedicate time to body scanning, where you mentally check in with each part of your body from head to toe. This promotes a comprehensive awareness of your body.

Stretching and Flexibility: Engage in stretching exercises to explore your body's range of motion. Pay attention to how your muscles lengthen and contract during stretching.

Daily Reflection: Set aside a few minutes each day for reflection on your body awareness journey. Consider any changes or discoveries you've made about your body.

FINAL THOUGHTS

In this enlightening chapter, we've ventured into the realm of body awareness and mindfulness, uncovering their profound impacts on both our physical and mental well-being. Through exploring the fundamentals of body awareness and immersing ourselves in various techniques, such as mindful breathing and guided imagery, you've gained a repertoire of powerful tools to cultivate a resilient mind-body connection.

As we conclude this chapter, it's crucial to recognize that the true magic lies not just in knowledge but in the application of these practices in your daily life. I urge you to take those initial steps toward incorporating these techniques into your routine. Remember, small changes can lead to significant transformations.

Our journey doesn't end here. In the upcoming chapter, we'll embark on a deeper exploration of the mind-body connection. Beyond awareness, we'll delve into the pivotal role it plays in fortifying your resilience against life's emotional trials. Brace yourself for an exciting continuation of our exploration as we continue to unlock the boundless potential of your mind and body.

CHAPTER FIVE

FOSTERING A DEEPER SOMATIC JOURNEY

 Self-care is how you take your power back.

— LAILA DELIA, SPIRITUAL AUTHOR

A key element of somatic therapy is recognizing self-care as a vital step toward harnessing our inner strength and embarking on a healing journey. Somatic practices offer a powerful pathway to reclaiming personal power, grounding this journey in the body's inherent wisdom. By integrating somatic theory, we unlock a deeper understanding of self-care as a dynamic process of healing and empowerment, reflecting fluidity and depth in our quest for holistic well-being.

ADVANCED TECHNIQUES FOR ADDRESSING DEEPER TENSIONS

Many of our tensions run deep due to the intricate interplay between past experiences, emotional patterns, and ingrained bodily responses, introducing the need for sophisticated somatic techniques to unravel and address them effectively. Exploring advanced techniques in somatic therapy addresses these deeper tensions and maximizes healing.

Here are some of the most popular and effective techniques that are designed to address and alleviate these deeper tensions:

Progressive Muscle Relaxation

Progressive muscle relaxation (PMR) is a powerful technique used in somatic therapy to address both physical and emotional tensions. It offers a direct approach to tackling the fight/flight/freeze response, allowing individuals to release built-up stress and anxiety stored within their bodies. By targeting the physical symptoms directly, PMR helps to free up mental energy, enabling individuals to address other symptoms more effectively.

The essence of PMR lies in its ability to systematically tense and then relax each muscle group in the body. This exercise is designed to reduce stress and promote relaxation by inducing a state of deep muscular relaxation. As individuals progressively tense and release their muscles, they become more attuned to the sensations of tension and relaxation within their bodies.

The theory behind PMR is grounded in the principle that it is impossible to experience both relaxation and anxiety simultane-ously. By deliberately inducing relaxation in the muscles, individ-uals disrupt the physiological processes associated with anxiety, such as increased heart rate and shallow breathing. As a result, they experience a sense of calm and well-being that counteracts the symptoms of anxiety.

One of the key benefits of PMR is its capacity to enhance body awareness and self-regulation skills. Through regular practice, individuals develop a heightened awareness of tension patterns within their bodies, allowing them to intervene and release tension before it escalates into full-blown anxiety. Additionally, PMR cultivates a sense of agency and control over one's physiological responses, empowering individuals to manage stress more effectively in their daily lives.

Step-by-Step Instructions for Practicing PMR

This exercise does wonders to melt pent-up tension.

Step 1: Find a quiet and comfortable space where you can lie down or sit in a relaxed position.

Step 2: Close your eyes and take a few deep breaths to center yourself and bring your awareness to the present moment.

Step 3: Starting with your feet, deliberately tense the muscles in your toes and feet, holding the tension for one minute.

Step 4: Release the tension in your feet and allow them to relax completely, noticing the sensation of relaxation spreading throughout your lower limbs.

Step 5: Gradually move your focus upward, tensing and relaxing each muscle group in sequence, including your calves, thighs, buttocks, abdomen, chest, arms, hands, shoulders, neck, and face. Hold each for one minute as you do so.

Step 6: As you tense each muscle group, focus on the sensation of tension building and then consciously release it, allowing the muscles to become loose and limp.

Step 7: Continue this process, moving systematically through each muscle group in your body until you have tensed and relaxed all major muscle groups.

Step 8: Take five minutes to rest and enjoy the deep sense of relaxation that follows, noticing how your body feels lighter and more at ease.

Sometimes, tension is lurking on an even deeper physical level. The next technique addresses such issues.

Deep Tissue Massage

Deep tissue massage is a therapeutic technique that focuses on reaching deeper layers of muscles and connective tissue. It's designed to release chronic tension and knots, promoting relaxation and alleviating pain. Here's a detailed overview of deep tissue massage, including its benefits and step-by-step instructions for practicing it:

Deep tissue massage involves applying firm pressure and slow strokes to target deep layers of muscles and connective tissue. Unlike traditional Swedish massage, which primarily focuses on relaxation, deep tissue massage aims to address specific areas that tend to store stress. It is a therapeutic technique that targets deep layers of muscles and connective tissues to alleviate chronic tension and pain. Unlike Swedish massage, which focuses on relaxation, deep tissue massage aims to address specific issues, such as muscle knots and tension areas. Therapists apply firm pressure and slow strokes using their hands, forearms, elbows, and occasionally tools to release knots and break up muscle tightness.

Somatic Benefits of Deep Tissue Massage

Deep tissue massage is seamlessly integrated into somatic therapy as a means to address deep-seated physical and emotional tensions. By targeting the deeper layers of muscles and connective tissue, this therapeutic technique not only releases chronic tension and knots but also facilitates the release of stored emotional stress.

Through the application of firm pressure and slow strokes, deep tissue massage helps individuals become more attuned to their bodily sensations and promotes a deeper sense of embodiment. This integration within somatic therapy allows individuals to explore and release both physical and emotional tension, fostering holistic healing and well-being. Below, you'll learn how to give a deep tissue massage:

Step-by-Step Instructions for Deep Tissue Massage with Somatic Intentions

By following the step-by-step instructions below, practitioners can effectively perform deep tissue massage to address specific issues and promote overall well-being for clients.

Step 1: Preparation

Before starting the massage, ensure the client is comfortably positioned on a massage table or mat, lying face down.

Step 2: Warm-Up

Apply a small amount of massage oil or lotion to your hands to reduce friction. Begin with light effleurage strokes to warm up the muscles and prepare them for deeper work.

Step 3: Identify Target Areas

Identify areas of tension or discomfort in the client's body, focusing on specific muscle groups or regions where deep pressure is needed.

Step 4: Apply Firm Pressure

Using your thumbs, knuckles, or elbows, apply firm pressure to the targeted muscles, gradually increasing depth as tolerated by the client. Communicate with the client to ensure the pressure is within their comfort level.

Step 5: Slow, Deep Strokes

Use slow, deliberate strokes to work through layers of muscle tissue, following the natural grain of the muscles. Maintain a consistent rhythm and pressure throughout the massage.

Step 6: Address Knots and Adhesions

Pay particular attention to areas of muscle knots or adhesions, applying sustained pressure, and using cross-fiber friction or stripping techniques to break up adhesions and release tension.

Step 8: Gradual Release

As the massage progresses, pressure is gradually released, and lighter strokes are transitioned to promote relaxation and integration of the work.

Step 9: Complete the Session

Finish the massage with a few minutes of light effleurage strokes to soothe the muscles and promote relaxation. Offer the client water and encourage them to rest and hydrate following the session.

Trauma-Informed Yoga

As mentioned in Chapter 1, trauma-informed yoga is a specialized approach to yoga practice that recognizes the widespread impact of trauma on the body and mind. It emphasizes creating a safe and supportive environment enabling individuals to explore bodily sensations while minimizing the risk of re-traumatization. Unlike traditional yoga, which may focus solely on physical postures, trauma-informed yoga integrates mindfulness, breathwork, and gentle movement to promote healing and empowerment.

Key Differences from Typical Yoga

- **Emphasis on Safety:** Trauma-informed yoga prioritizes creating a safe space for individuals, acknowledging that traumatic experiences can lead to feelings of vulnerability and discomfort.
- **Choice and Agency**: Unlike traditional yoga classes that may encourage individuals to push their limits, trauma-informed yoga emphasizes choice and agency, empowering individuals to make decisions based on their comfort level.
- **Sensory Awareness**: Trauma-informed yoga encourages individuals to cultivate awareness of their bodily sensations without judgment, allowing them to reconnect with themselves in a gentle and compassionate manner.

While yoga can be a powerful tool for healing, it's essential to approach it with caution, especially in the context of trauma. Certain poses and practices may inadvertently trigger traumatic responses or exacerbate existing symptoms. Here are some practices to avoid in trauma-informed yoga:

- **Forced Poses:** Avoid poses that require deep stretching or forceful movements, as they can evoke feelings of vulnerability and discomfort.
- **Fast-Paced Sequences**: Avoid rapid transitions between poses or sequences that may overwhelm individuals, leading to increased anxiety or dissociation.
- **Invasive Touch:** Refrain from hands-on adjustments or physical assists without explicit consent, as they can trigger feelings of invasion or distress.
- **Specific Poses (adjust on an individual basis)**: It's essential to offer modifications and alternatives, allowing each individual to find their own space of safety and comfort, based on the varied experiences of each person. Use props for support or adapt the pose to suit their comfort levels.

Step-by-Step Instructions for Trauma-Informed Yoga Techniques

Now, let's explore some trauma-informed yoga techniques that practitioners can incorporate into their practice:

1. Grounding Poses

Step 1: Begin in a comfortable seated position on your mat, with your spine tall and your hands resting gently on your knees or thighs.

Step 2: Close your eyes if comfortable, or soften your gaze, and take a few deep breaths to center yourself.

Step 3: When ready, transition from your seated position into child's pose. Place your hands on the ground in front of you and slowly lower your forehead down, resting it on the mat in child's pose. Adjust this pose as needed to accommodate and respect the varied experiences of each trauma survivor.

Step 4: Press your palms firmly into the ground, feeling the support beneath you, and allow your hips to sink toward your heels.

Step 5: Stay in this pose for several breaths, focusing on the sensation of grounding and stability beneath you.

2. Gentle Movement

Step 1: From child's pose, gently rise up to a seated position on your heels, bringing your hands to your heart center in prayer position, and count to thirty.

Step 2: On an inhale, sweep your arms overhead, reaching up toward the sky, and lengthen through your spine for one minute.

Step 3: On an exhale, slowly twist to the right, bringing your left hand to your right knee and your right hand behind you for support, and count to thirty.

Step 4: Inhale to lengthen through your spine and exhale to deepen the twist, gazing over your right shoulder if comfortable. Again, count to thirty.

Step 5: Hold the twist for a few breaths, then inhale to come back to center and repeat on the other side.

3. Breath Awareness

Step 1: Find a comfortable seated or reclined position on your mat, allowing your spine to be long and your body to relax for 2 minutes.

Step 2: Close your eyes if comfortable, or soften your gaze, and bring your awareness to your breath.

Step 3: Notice the natural rhythm of your breath without trying to change it, simply observing the rise and fall of your chest and abdomen.

Step 4: As you continue to breathe, begin to deepen your inhalations and exhalations, allowing each breath to be full and complete.

Step 5: With each inhale, envision yourself drawing in peace and calm, and with each exhale, release any tension or stress you may be holding onto.

4. Somatic Experiencing

Step 1: Find a comfortable position, sitting or lying down, in a safe and quiet environment.

Step 2: Begin by noticing your breath without trying to change it. Observe the natural rhythm of your breathing as you settle into the present moment.

Step 3: Gently bring your attention to any physical sensations in your body. This could be the feeling of your feet on the ground, the weight of your body on the chair, or the temperature of the air against your skin.

Step 4: As you notice sensations, observe any emotional responses or thoughts that arise without trying to alter them. The goal is not to change these sensations but to witness and validate your experience.

Step 5: If you identify areas where you feel stuck or heightened sensation, allow yourself to make small, comfortable movements or adjustments that promote a sense of relief or release. This could involve gently shifting your posture, stretching slightly, or touching a part of your body in a reassuring way.

Step 6: Continue this mindful observation, letting the process unfold organically. The key is to engage with what you feel and experience, allowing the nervous system to naturally adjust and regulate itself.

Step 7: Whenever you feel overwhelmed, return your focus to grounding sensations, such as the feel of the ground under you or the air entering your nostrils, to help stabilize your experience.

Step 8: Conclude the session by reflecting on any changes in your body or emotional state, acknowledging any shifts, no matter how small, towards greater ease or clarity.

5. Self-Compassion

Step 1: Find a comfortable seated or reclined position on your mat, allowing your body to relax and your breath to be natural.

Step 2: Place one hand on your heart and the other hand on your belly, connecting with the warmth and comfort of your own touch.

Step 3: Take a few deep breaths, allowing yourself to feel supported and held by your own presence.

Step 4: Repeat a compassionate mantra or affirmation to yourself, such as "May I be safe, may I be happy, may I be healthy, may I be at peace."

Step 5: Take as much time as you need in this nurturing space, allowing yourself to receive the love and compassion you deserve.

Imagery Tracking (Somatic ImageryTM)

Somatic imagery, also known as imagery tracking or somatic tracking, is a dynamic therapeutic modality that delves deep into the multi-sensory and somatic dimensions of imagery. Unlike tradi-tional visualization techniques, Somatic Imagery™ enhances the power of the experience, accessing a wealth of sensory information and unlocking the potential for profound change. It operates on an intuitive and creative level, bypassing defenses and resistance with gentle effectiveness, making it a potent catalyst for transformation.

Understanding the Power of Somatic ImageryTM:

Somatic Imagery™ offers a unique approach to healing, over-coming feelings of powerlessness and hopelessness by tapping into the body's innate wisdom. By engaging both the mind and body in the therapeutic process, this modality facilitates shifts in entrenched thinking and behavior patterns, paving the way for profound healing and growth.

Benefits of Somatic ImageryTM:

- **Enhanced Multi-Sensory Experience**: Somatic Imagery™ enriches the therapeutic experience by engaging all the senses, creating a more vivid and immersive journey toward healing.
- **Increased Potential for Change**: By accessing deeper layers of consciousness, Somatic Imagery™ opens the door to transformation, allowing individuals to break free from limiting beliefs and behaviors.
- **Gentle and Noninvasive**: Somatic Imagery™ gently bypasses defenses and resistance, fostering a safe and supportive environment for exploration and healing.

Exploring Somatic Imagery for Pain Relief

Somatic imagery is a specialized technique aimed at retraining the brain's response to signals from the body, particularly in the context of chronic pain. It involves exposing individuals to pain sensations in a safe and controlled manner, with the goal of gradually desensitizing their response and restoring a sense of safety and control.

Understanding the Process of Somatic Imagery

In somatic imagery, individuals are guided to tune into their bodily sensations and observe them without judgment or fear. Through repeated exposure to these sensations in a safe environment, individuals learn to reinterpret the signals from their bodies, gradually reducing the intensity of their pain response over time.

Some of the greatest benefits of somatic imagery include:

- **Retraining the Brain**: Somatic imagery helps individuals break free from the cycle of chronic pain by rewiring neural pathways associated with pain perception.
- **Promoting Safety and Control:** By exposing individuals to pain sensations in a safe and supportive environment, somatic imagery helps restore a sense of empowerment.
- **Facilitating Long-Term Relief**: While the immediate goal of somatic imagery is to help individuals feel safe in the presence of pain, the ultimate aim is to reduce pain sensations over the long term through repeated exposure and reconditioning of the brain's response.

Step-by-Step Instructions for Imagery Tracking

Step 1: Find a Quiet and Comfortable Space

Begin by locating a quiet and comfortable space where you can fully focus on the imagery tracking process. This environment should be free from distractions, allowing you to immerse yourself in the experience.

Step 2: Relax Your Body and Mind

Take a few deep breaths to center yourself and relax your body and mind. Release any tension or stress you may be holding onto, allowing yourself to enter a state of deep relaxation.

Step 3: Set an Intention

Before starting the imagery tracking practice, set an intention for what you hope to explore or achieve. This intention will guide your experience and provide a framework for your imagery journey.

Step 4: Begin the Imagery Journey

Close your eyes and begin to visualize a peaceful and serene scene or image. Engage all your senses to make the imagery as vivid and immersive as possible. Notice the sights, sounds, smells, textures, and even tastes associated with your chosen imagery.

Step 5: Explore Sensations in the Body

As you continue with the imagery journey, pay attention to any sensations or feelings that arise in your body. Notice where tension or discomfort may be present, and allow yourself to fully experience these sensations without judgment.

Step 6: Release and Transform

With each breath, imagine releasing any tension or discomfort from your body, allowing it to dissolve and transform into a sense of relaxation and well-being. Visualize this process unfolding with each inhale and exhale, gradually releasing any blocks or resistance.

Step 7: Reflect and Integrate

Take a few moments to reflect on your imagery experience and how it has impacted you. Notice any shifts or insights that may have occurred during the practice. Allow these insights to integrate into your awareness, carrying them forward into your daily life.

EDMR and Bilateral Stimulation

Bilateral stimulation serves as a fundamental component of eye movement desensitization and reprocessing (EMDR) therapy, renowned for its efficacy in trauma treatment. This technique entails the use of stimuli—visual, auditory, or tactile—that follow a rhythmic left-right pattern. For instance, visual bilateral stimulation may involve tracking a hand or moving light as it alternates between the left and right fields of vision. Similarly, auditory bilateral stimulation could entail listening to tones that oscillate between the left and right sides of the head.

Bilateral stimulation plays a pivotal role in inhibiting the amygdala, a key brain region associated with fear and the fight-or-flight response. By engaging in bilateral tapping or shifting the eyes back and forth, individuals can effectively suppress this fear response, thereby mitigating the physiological arousal commonly linked to traumatic or distressing memories.

Step-by-Step Instructions for Bilateral Stimulation

Step 1: Set the Stage

Create a quiet and comfortable environment conducive to relaxation and focus. Eliminate any potential distractions to ensure an optimal therapeutic experience.

Step 2: Choose Your Modality

Select the type of bilateral stimulation that resonates most with you—whether visual, auditory, or tactile. Experiment with different modalities to determine which one feels most effective for your needs.

Step 3: Establish Rhythmic Movement

Initiate the bilateral stimulation by implementing a rhythmic left-right pattern. For visual stimulation, this could involve tracking a hand or moving light as it oscillates from left to right and back again. Alternatively, for auditory stimulation, listen to tones that alternate between the left and right sides of the head.

Step 4: Focus on Sensations

As you engage in bilateral stimulation, pay close attention to any sensations or experiences that arise within your body and mind. Notice any shifts in emotional or physiological states as you continue the practice.

Step 5: Allow Processing to Occur

Trust in the innate healing capacity of your mind and body as you engage in bilateral stimulation. Allow any thoughts, feelings, or memories to surface and be processed in a safe and supportive manner.

Step 6: Reflect and Integrate

Following the bilateral stimulation session, take a moment to reflect on your experience and any insights gained. Allow these insights to integrate into your awareness, fostering a sense of empowerment and resilience in the face of past traumas or challenges.

REAL LIFE CASE STUDIES

EMDR: Meg's Miracle

In 2023, Meg Weber shared her transformative journey with EMDR therapy, initially seeking healing from her sister's suicide and other personal traumas. Upon experiencing significant relief and understanding the power of EMDR firsthand, Weber decided to extend this healing tool to her clients. She recounts the stark transition from casual introductory questions to deep, therapeutic inquiries on her first day at a trauma retreat, setting the stage for intensive EMDR sessions. Weber's narrative includes confronting memories of loss, betrayal, and personal hardship, with EMDR facilitating a process less about conversation and more about directly engaging with and processing traumatic memories. The therapy, typically involving eye movements, was adapted to her needs with tactile feedback devices, allowing her to focus inwardly on painful memories and emotions. This approach led to profound moments of insight and emotional release, ultimately offering Weber not just a path through her grief and trauma but also a tool she could use to guide others through their healing. Completing her clinical training, Weber now practices EMDR, grateful for the empathy and understanding her personal journey allows her to bring to her clients, helping them navigate their traumas toward relief and liberation.

Deep Tissue Massage: Debra's Saving Grace

Debra's transition from enduring chronic tension due to a high-stress career to finding relief through deep tissue massage and somatic release was transformative. Initially skeptical, she discovered profound relief and emotional release under the skilled hands of her therapist, who employed deep tissue techniques to unravel physical knots and somatic practices to address the emotional underpinnings of her discomfort. This holistic approach not only alleviated her physical pain but also taught her the importance of listening to her body's signals, bridging the gap between her physical and emotional well-being. The journey led Debra to a deeper understanding of herself, fostering a balance that enriched her life in unforeseen ways. Her experience became a beacon for others, advocating the intertwined healing of body and mind through these therapeutic modalities.

DEVELOPING A PERSONAL SOMATIC YOGA ROUTINE FOR DIFFERENT TIMES OF THE DAY

Creating a personal somatic yoga routine tailored for different times of the day can significantly enhance your well-being, energy levels, and peace of mind. Below, you'll find detailed step-by-step instructions for developing morning and evening yoga practices designed to energize you at the start of your day and help you unwind before bed.

The eighteen basic yoga poses, often referred to as asanas, serve as the foundation for many yoga practices, offering a balanced mix of flexibility, strength, and relaxation. They are as follows:

- **Mountain Pose** (Tadasana): The foundational standing poses from which all others stem, promoting posture and balance.
- **Downward-Facing Dog** (Adho Mukha Svanasana): An essential pose for stretching the shoulders, hamstrings, calves, and hands.
- **Warrior I** (Virabhadrasana I): A powerful standing pose

that strengthens the legs and arms while opening up the chest and hips.

- **Warrior II** (Virabhadrasana II): Builds lower body strength and stamina and improves concentration and balance.
- **Triangle Pose** (Trikonasana): Stretches and strengthens the thighs, knees, and ankles while reducing stress and anxiety.
- **Tree Pose** (Vrksasana): Improves balance and stability in the legs while also toning the abdominal muscles.
- **Chair Pose** (Utkatasana): Strengthens the ankles, thighs, calves, and spine while stretching shoulders and chest.
- **Child's Pose** (Balasana): A restorative, calming pose that stretches the hips, thighs, and ankles, relieving stress and fatigue.
- **Cat-Cow Stretch** (Marjaryasana-Bitilasana): A gentle flow between two poses that warms up the spine and relieves back tension.
- **Cobra Pose** (Bhujangasana): Strengthens the spine, shoulders, and buttocks while stretching the chest, lungs, shoulders, and abdomen.
- **Seated Forward Bend** (Paschimottanasana): Calms the brain, relieves stress, and stretches the spine, shoulders, and hamstrings.
- **Bridge Pose** (Setu Bandhasana): A backbend that strengthens the back muscles, stretches the chest, neck, and spine, and can alleviate stress and mild depression.
- **Boat Pose** (Navasana): Strengthens the abdomen, hip flexors, and spine while stimulating the kidneys, thyroid and prostate glands, and intestines.
- **Plank Pose**: Builds strength in the core, shoulders, arms, and legs and enhances stamina.
- **Four-Limbed Staff Pose** (Chaturanga Dandasana):

Strengthens the arms and wrists, tones the abdomen, and prepares the body for more challenging arm balances.

- **Warrior III** (Virabhadrasana III): A balancing pose that strengthens the legs, tones the abdomen, improves balance and posture, and can help focus the mind.
- **Half Lord of the Fishes Pose** (Ardha Matsyendrasana): Increases spinal flexibility, stretches the shoulders and hips, and tones the abdomen.

You'll find a detailed guide with some of these poses in my bonus *Yoga Bliss in 10 minutes: Effortless Somatic Practices for Daily Wellness*, which also includes a daily stress symptom checklist.

Morning Routine

Incorporating yoga into your morning routine offers unique benefits that specifically cater to starting your day on the right note. Here are eight somatic benefits of engaging in morning yoga:

Energizes the Body: Morning yoga helps shake off sleep inertia and invigorates your body, preparing you for the day ahead with increased energy and alertness.

Stimulates Digestive System: Gentle stretches and twists can help wake up the digestive tract, promoting healthy bowel movement and metabolism early in the day.

Boosts Mental Clarity: Practicing yoga in the morning clears the mind, reduces morning fog, and enhances concentration and cognitive function for the day's tasks.

Sets a Positive Tone for the Day: Starting your day with yoga can improve your mood and set a foundation of calm and focus that influences how you navigate daily challenges.

Improves Circulation: Morning yoga gets the blood flowing after a night of rest, delivering oxygen and nutrients more effectively throughout the body.

Enhances Flexibility and Mobility: Morning stretches can alleviate stiffness from sleeping, improve flexibility and mobility, and prepare your muscles and joints for daily activities.

Balances Hormones: Yoga can help balance hormone levels, including cortisol, the stress hormone, which naturally peaks in the morning. This can lead to a more balanced emotional state throughout the day.

Strengthens Immune System: The combination of physical movement and deep breathing in yoga can help stimulate lymphatic flow, which supports the body's immune functions.

Step-by-Step Instructions

Begin with Mountain Pose (Tadasana): Stand with your feet hip-width apart, arms at your sides. Inhale deeply, raising your arms overhead, palms facing each other. Exhale slowly, grounding your feet into the earth. Hold for 3–5 breaths. This pose promotes balance and grounding.

Transition to Cat and Cow Pose (Marjaryasana and Bitilasana): Get on all fours, ensuring your knees are under your hips and your wrists are under your shoulders. Inhale as you arch your back, looking upward (Cow Pose), and exhale as you round your spine, tucking your chin to your chest (Cat Pose). Repeat for 5–7 cycles, synchronizing your movement with your breath. This warms up the spine and relieves stiffness.

Move into Child's Pose (Balasana): Sit back on your heels, stretch your arms forward, and lower your forehead to the ground. Hold for 5–10 breaths. This pose is calming and stretches the back.

Proceed to Downward Facing Dog (Adho Mukha Svanasana): From all fours, lift your hips up and back, straighten your legs as much as possible, and push your hands into the ground. Hold for 5–8 breaths. This pose energizes the body and stretches the hamstrings.

Flow into Sun Salutation A (Surya Namaskar A): Sun Salutation A (Surya Namaskar A) is a fundamental yoga sequence that consists of a flow of 12 poses performed in a graceful, continuous cycle, synchronized with the breath. This series is designed to build heat in the body, improve circulation, and increase flexibility and strength. It's often used as a warm-up at the beginning of a yoga practice, but it can also serve as a complete practice on its own. Here's a brief overview of the sequence:

Mountain Pose (Tadasana): Stand with feet together, arms by the sides, engaging your core and thighs with a neutral spine. Draw your navel towards your spine, and open your chest with your arms at your sides.

Upward Salute (Urdhva Hastasana): Inhale and extend your arms overhead, palms touching; gently arch back if comfortable and look up toward your hands.

Forward Fold (Uttanasana): Exhale and hinge at the hips to fold forward, placing your hands beside your feet. Relax your neck and let your head hang heavily.

Halfway Lift (Ardha Uttanasana): Inhale and lift your torso halfway up, lengthening the spine, hands on shins, or thighs, ensuring you back is flat.

Plank Pose: Exhale, step, or jump back to plank pose, aligning your shoulders over your wrists and body in a straight line from head to heels.

Four-Limbed Staff Pose: Chaturanga Dandasana: Lower to a half push-up, keeping elbows close to the body.

Upward-Facing Dog (Urdhva Mukha Svanasana): Inhale and straighten the arms, lifting the chest and thighs off the floor, shoulders back and look up.

Downward-Facing Dog (Adho Mukha Svanasana): Exhale and lift the hips up and back, forming an inverted V-shape. Keep your hands and feet firmly planted as you lengthen your spine and relax your neck.

Return to Forward Fold (Uttanasana): Inhale and fold deeply into the pose.

Return to Halfway Lift (Ardha Uttanasana): Inhale and lift your torso halfway up again, lengthening the spine, hands on shins, or thighs, ensuring you back is flat.

Return to Upward Salute (Urdhva Hastasana): Inhale, rise to stand, sweep arms overhead, and gently arch back.

Mountain Pose (Tadasana): Exhale and return to mountain pose with arms by the sides.

Sun salutation A is typically performed several times in a row to build warmth and prepare the body for more intense asanas that might follow in a yoga sequence. It's essential to focus on the breath, allowing inhalations to lift or open the body and exhalations to fold or ground. Perform 3–5 rounds, focusing on fluid movement and breath.

Incorporate a Gentle Twist with Seated Spinal Twist (Ardha Matsyendrasana): Sit with your legs extended, bend your right knee over the left leg, and twist your torso to the right, placing your right hand behind you for support. Hold for five breaths, then switch sides. Twists are detoxifying and stimulate digestion.

End with a Forward Fold to Calm the Nervous System: Seated Forward Fold (Paschimottanasana) or Standing Forward Fold (Uttanasana) as follows:

Seated Forward Fold (Paschimottanasana)

Step-by-Step Instructions

Start Seated: Begin by sitting on the floor with your legs stretched out in front of you. Keep your spine erect and toes flexed toward you.

Inhale and Stretch: Inhale deeply and raise your arms overhead, stretching the spine up long.

Exhale and Fold: As you exhale, hinge from your hips and fold forward. Aim to move your torso over your legs rather than simply reaching down to your toes. Keep the spine elongated.

Reach Your Feet: Extend your hands toward your feet. If you can, hold the sides of your feet with your hands. If not, hold onto your shins or ankles. The key is to maintain the integrity of the stretch in your spine and hamstrings, not necessarily to reach your feet.

Deepen the Pose: With each exhale, gently deepen the fold, bringing your torso closer to your legs. Avoid rounding the back. Think of lengthening the front of your torso.

Hold the Pose: Stay in this position for 3–5 breaths, or as long as comfortable, deepening the stretch with each exhalation. Keep your shoulders relaxed and away from your ears.

Release: To come out of the pose, inhale and lift your torso up slowly. As you exhale, lower your arms back to your sides.

Tips

- It's more important to keep your spine straight and long than to reach your toes.
- Use a yoga strap around your feet if you can't reach them comfortably.

Standing Forward Fold (*Uttanasana*)

Step-by-Step Instructions: Standing Forward Fold

Start by Standing: Begin in Mountain Pose (Tadasana), standing with your feet hip-width apart and arms by your sides.

Inhale and Prepare: Take a deep breath in and extend your arms out to the sides and overhead, stretching up through your spine.

Exhale and Fold: As you exhale, hinge at your hips to fold forward, keeping your spine and legs straight as you come down.

Hands to Feet: Place your hands on the ground beside your feet, on your shins, or grasp the back of your ankles, depending on your flexibility. Let your head hang naturally.

Deepen the Pose: With each exhale, allow your body to fold deeper. Keep your hips over your ankles, and if possible, press your palms flat against the floor.

Hold the Pose: Maintain the pose for a few breaths, focusing on lengthening your spine with each inhale and deepening the fold with each exhale.

Release: To come out of the pose, inhale and slowly rise back up to standing, leading with your chest and keeping your back straight. Finally, return to mountain pose.

Tips

- Keep a slight bend in your knees if you feel any strain on your lower back or hamstrings.
- Let your head hang freely to relax your neck and shoulders.
- Throughout your morning practice, focus on deep, mindful breathing to enhance the energizing effects of the poses and prepare mentally for the day ahead.

Evening Routine

The objective of this routine is to release the day's stress, wind down, and prepare for a restful night's sleep.

Start with Gentle Seated Twists: To relax the spine and calm the nervous system. Sit comfortably, inhale tall, and on an exhale, gently twist to one side. Hold for five breaths, then switch sides.

Move into Forward Bends: Like Seated Forward Fold (Paschimottanasana) or Child's Pose (Balasana) for 5–10 breaths to soothe the mind and stretch the back.

Incorporate Leg-Up-the-Wall Pose (Viparita Karani): Lie on your back and extend your legs up against a wall. This inversion is deeply relaxing and can help reduce anxiety.

Practice Gentle Hip Openers: Like Pigeon Pose (Eka Pada Rajakapotasana) for 5–10 breaths each side to release tension from the hips, where stress and emotions are often stored. Instructions include:

Pigeon Pose (Eka Pada Rajakapotasana)

Start in All-Fours: Begin on your hands and knees in a tabletop position.

Slide Foot Forward: Slide your right knee forward toward your right hand. Angle your right knee at two o'clock.

Extend Left Leg: Slowly extend your left leg back, keeping your hips square to the floor.

Adjust Position: Sit up straight to feel a stretch in your right hip. Use a cushion under your right hip for support if needed.

Fold Forward (optional): For a deeper stretch, fold forward over your right leg, extending your arms in front of you.

Hold and Breathe: Maintain the pose for 5–10 breaths, relaxing into the stretch.

Switch Sides: Gently release and repeat on the other side.

End with a Restorative Pose: Such as Supported Bridge Pose (Setu Bandha Sarvangasana) as instructed below with a yoga block under the sacrum for 5–10 minutes. This pose calms the nervous system and promotes relaxation.

Supported Bridge Pose

Prepare Your Support: Gather a yoga block or a firm, folded blanket as support for your lower back.

Start Position: Lie on your back with your knees bent and feet flat on the floor, hip-width apart. Place your arms by your sides, palms down.

Lift into Bridge: Press your feet and arms into the floor to lift your hips toward the ceiling.

Place Support: Carefully slide the yoga block or folded blanket under your sacrum (the flat area at the base of your spine). Adjust the height according to your comfort—higher for more intensity, lower for a gentler lift.

Adjust and Relax: Once the support is in place, adjust your position so that you feel comfortable and supported. Your weight should be resting on the block or blanket, not on your neck or shoulders.

Focus on Breath: With your hips supported, allow your body to relax into the pose. Breathe deeply and evenly, letting each exhale gently release any tension in your back and hips.

Leg Variation (Optional): For a deeper stretch, you may extend your legs one at a time to straighten them along the floor. This intensifies the stretch but is optional based on your comfort and flexibility.

Hold the Pose: Stay in supported bridge pose for 1 to 3 minutes, focusing on deep, relaxed breathing.

To Release: To come out of the pose, first lift your hips slightly to remove the block or blanket. Then, slowly lower your hips to the floor. Hug your knees into your chest for a gentle release before stretching out.

Rest: Allow yourself a moment in a neutral position, such as lying flat or in a fetal position, to let your body absorb the benefits of the pose.

Yoga Block under the Sacrum

Using a yoga block under the sacrum can enhance various yoga poses by providing support, increasing comfort, and deepening stretches. Here's how to effectively use a yoga block for sacral support:

Choose the Right Block: Select a yoga block that feels comfortable in terms of material and size. Foam blocks are great for comfort, while cork or wood blocks offer more stability.

Positioning the Block: While lying on your back with knees bent and feet flat on the floor, lift your hips slightly. Slide the yoga block under your sacrum, the triangular bone at the base of your spine. Ensure the block is positioned securely and provides a comfortable lift.

Adjust the Height: Yoga blocks typically have three height settings —low, medium, and high. Start with the lowest height to see how it feels. You can adjust the height for more or less support as needed. The higher the block, the more intense the stretch or lift.

Enter the Pose: Once the block is in place, adjust your legs according to the specific pose you're practicing. For a restorative version of bridge pose, you might keep your knees bent and feet flat. For a deeper hip or lower back stretch, you might straighten your legs or bring them into a bound angle position with the soles of your feet together and knees wide apart.

Focus on Relaxation and Breathing: With the block supporting your sacrum, allow your body to relax over and around the block. Take deep, even breaths, letting each exhale help you release tension.

To Release: Carefully lift your hips, remove the block, and lower your sacrum back to the floor. Pause for a moment to feel the effects of the pose before moving on.

Other helpful evening poses include:

- **Reclining Hand-to-Big-Toe Pose (Supta Padangusthasana):** Lie on your back, lift one leg, and hold your big toe with your hand or a yoga strap. This pose stretches the hamstrings and calms the mind, aiding in relaxation before sleep.
- **Supine Spinal Twist (Supta Matsyendrasana):** Lying on your back, bring your knees to one side while turning your head to the opposite direction. This gentle twist helps to release tension in the spine and relax the nervous system.
- **Savasana (Corpse Pose):** End your routine by lying flat on your back with your arms and legs comfortably spread apart. Close your eyes and breathe deeply, allowing your body and mind to completely relax. Savasana helps to reduce stress, calm the mind, and prepare the body for sleep.

Incorporating these poses into your evening routine can further help to unwind and destress, promoting a deep and restorative sleep.

Conclude with a Mindfulness Practice or Meditation: Focus on deep, slow breathing or a guided sleep meditation to quiet the mind and ease into a state conducive to sleep.

For both routines, remember to listen to your body, adjusting poses and durations to suit your needs. The objective is not perfection but presence and awareness, fostering a harmonious balance between mind and body. These practices, derived from traditional yoga and modern mindfulness techniques, are designed to support your journey toward holistic health and well-being.

Incorporating mindfulness into your evening routine can significantly enhance the quality of your sleep. Mindfulness practices help calm the mind, reduce stress, and alleviate anxiety, creating the ideal mental state for a restful night. By focusing on the present moment and acknowledging but not engaging with distracting thoughts, mindfulness can break the cycle of worry and tension that often leads to insomnia.

Why Practice Mindfulness for Sleep

- **Reduces Stress**: Mindfulness lowers cortisol levels, the stress hormone, promoting relaxation.
- **Improves Sleep Quality:** By calming the mind, mindfulness can lead to deeper, more restorative sleep.
- **Decreases Anxiety**: Regular mindfulness practice can diminish the anxiety that often disrupts sleep.
- **Enhances Relaxation**: Focusing on the present moment can help ease the body into a state of relaxation, making it easier to fall asleep.

Mindfulness Dos for a Good Night's Sleep

- **Do Create a Mindful Bedtime Routine**: Engage in calming activities, such as reading or gentle yoga, to signal your body that it's time to wind down.
- **Do Practice Breathing Exercises:** Deep, slow breathing can reduce stress and prepare your body for sleep.
- **Do Keep a Gratitude Journal**: Spend a few minutes before bed reflecting on positive aspects of your day to cultivate a sense of contentment and peace.

- **Do Use Guided Meditation**: Listening to a guided sleep meditation can help redirect your focus from worrisome thoughts to relaxation.

Mindfulness Don'ts for a Good Night's Sleep

- **Don't Engage with Electronic Devices before Bed**: The blue light from screens can disrupt your sleep cycle, so avoid phones, tablets, and computers at least an hour before bedtime.
- **Don't Dwell on Negative Thoughts:** Acknowledge any negative thoughts that arise, but let them pass without engaging deeply with them.
- **Don't Practice Intense Exercise Too Close to Bedtime:** While physical activity is beneficial, engaging in it too close to bedtime can energize the body, making it harder to relax.
- **Don't Consume Caffeine Late in the Day**: Avoid coffee, tea, or other caffeinated beverages in the evening, as they can interfere with your ability to fall asleep.

Tailoring Your Somatic Approach to Individual Needs

Tailoring your somatic approach to individual needs is essential for maximizing the benefits of somatic practices, which include a range of body-centered activities designed to foster self-awareness, healing, and personal growth. To personalize these practices effectively, consider the following detailed strategies and insights from professionals in the field:

- **Start with Self-Assessment**: Begin by taking stock of your current physical and emotional state. Note any areas of tension, discomfort, or emotional unrest. This initial assessment will guide you in choosing the most appropriate somatic techniques.

- **Set Clear Intentions**: Identify what you hope to achieve through your somatic practice. Whether it's reducing stress, alleviating physical pain, or enhancing emotional resilience, having a clear goal can guide your choice of techniques.
- **Choose Techniques Wisely**: Select somatic practices that resonate with your physical and emotional needs. For instance, if you're dealing with stress, techniques focusing on breath work and gentle movement might be most beneficial.
- **Listen to Your Body:** Develop a deep listening practice to understand your body's signals. If a particular movement or technique increases discomfort or emotional distress, take it as a cue to modify or choose an alternative approach. Your body's response is a key indicator of what it needs at any given moment.
- **Adapt Practices Accordingly**: Be willing to adapt techniques based on your day-to-day experiences. Flexibility in your somatic practice allows you to address your changing needs, ensuring that the approach remains relevant and supportive.
- **Incorporate Mindfulness:** Engage in practices with mindfulness, focusing on the present moment and the sensations arising in your body. This heightened awareness can enhance the effectiveness of somatic techniques.
- **Seek Professional Guidance**: Consider consulting with a somatic therapist or yoga instructor who can offer personalized advice and adjustments. Their expertise can be invaluable in tailoring practices to your unique circumstances.

Insights from Professionals

Linda Graham, a somatic therapist, reminds us that "A self-compassionate response accepts your experiences and vulnerabilities as opportunities for proactive self-care." This perspective encourages individuals to personalize somatic practices as a form of self-compassion, addressing personal needs and experiences with kindness and understanding.

Thomas Hanna, the founder of Clinical Somatic Education, emphasizes the importance of personal experience, stating, "The human body is not an instrument to be used, but a realm of one's being to be experienced, explored, enriched, and, thereby, educated." Hanna's insight underscores the value of customizing somatic practices to deepen one's connection and understanding of your body.

Sarah Whatley, a dance and somatic movement expert, defines somatic practices as "body-based movement practices that foreground self-awareness and a first-person experience of moving." Whatley's definition highlights the importance of personalizing these practices to enhance self-awareness and the individual's unique experience of movement.

By incorporating these personalization strategies and embracing the wisdom shared by somatic professionals, you can develop a somatic practice that not only addresses your individual needs but also fosters a deeper connection with your body and mind.

Interactive Element

This exercise is designed to help you connect more deeply with your body and emotions by mapping how different emotions manifest physically within you. By recognizing and recording these sensations, you can gain insights into your emotional well-being and develop strategies to manage your emotions more effectively.

Step 1: Preparation

Gather Materials: You'll need a large sheet of paper (A3 or poster size), colored markers or pencils, and a quiet, comfortable space where you won't be disturbed.

Create a Comfortable Setting: Ensure the space is inviting and conducive to introspection. You might want to play soft, ambient music or light a candle.

Step 2: Creating Your Emotion Body Map

Draw an Outline of Your Body: On the large sheet of paper, draw a simple outline of a body. You can either trace around yourself with the help of a friend or draw a silhouette freehand.

Identify Emotions: Think about a range of emotions you commonly experience—both positive and negative—such as happiness, sadness, anxiety, love, anger, and peace.

Reflect on Physical Sensations: Close your eyes and recall a recent moment when you felt each emotion strongly. Notice where in your body you felt a physical response. Did your chest tighten with anxiety? Did your stomach flutter with excitement?

Step 3: Mapping Emotions to Body Sensations

Color Coding: Assign a color to each emotion. For example, red for anger, blue for sadness, and yellow for happiness.

Mark the Sensations: Using the corresponding colors, mark the areas on your body outline where you felt each emotion. Use symbols, shapes, or shading to represent different sensations, such as spirals for tension or stars for energy.

Add Annotations: Next to each marked area, write a brief note about the sensation. For example, "tightness in the chest when anxious" or "warmth in the heart when feeling love."

Step 4: Reflection and Analysis

Review Your Map: Take a step back and observe your emotion body map as a whole. Notice patterns or areas of your body that are particularly sensitive to certain emotions.

Reflect on Your Discoveries: Consider how this map reflects your emotional experiences. Are there emotions that manifest more physically than others? Are there surprises in how some emotions are embodied?

Journal Your Insights: In a journal or on the back of your map, write down any insights or thoughts about the connections between your emotions and physical sensations. Reflect on how this awareness can help you manage your emotions better.

Step 5: Integration and Application

Develop Awareness: Use your emotion body map as a tool to become more aware of your emotional states throughout the day. Recognizing the physical manifestations of your emotions early on can give you a head start in managing them.

Practice Mindful Breathing: When you notice a physical sensation associated with a challenging emotion, pause and practice mindful breathing. Focus on sending breath to that part of your body, imagining tension releasing with each exhale.

Create Coping Strategies: Based on your map, develop personalized coping strategies. For example, if tension accumulates in your shoulders with stress, incorporate shoulder stretches or massage into your daily routine.

This exercise is not only a powerful way to connect with your emotions and physical body but also a creative process that can offer profound insights into your emotional health. By regularly updating and reflecting on your emotion body map, you can deepen your self-awareness and enhance your emotional well-being.

FINAL THOUGHTS

As we wrap up this chapter, it's essential to recognize the personal journey you've embarked on by exploring the depths of somatic practices. The techniques and insights shared here, from progressive muscle relaxation to deep tissue massage and trauma-informed yoga, offer you powerful tools to navigate the complexities of your emotions and bodily sensations. By engaging with these practices, you're taking significant steps toward reclaiming your inner strength and embarking on a path of holistic healing.

This journey is deeply personal and uniquely yours. As you integrate these advanced techniques into your daily life, remember to listen to your body's wisdom and respond to its needs with compassion and mindfulness. The practice of somatic therapy is not just about addressing physical tensions; it's a profound exploration of the interconnectedness of your body and mind, leading to emotional resilience and empowerment.

Looking forward, the next chapter, "Somatic Therapy as an Alternative Path," promises to expand your understanding of how somatic therapy offers a distinctive approach to healing, different from traditional therapy methods. This exploration will provide you with further insights into alternative paths to well-being, encouraging you to continue your journey with an open heart and mind.

Don't forget, the path to healing and well-being is ongoing. Each step you take on this journey enriches your life with deeper awareness and a greater sense of balance. As you go forward, carry with you the lessons and practices from this chapter, allowing them to guide you toward a more connected and fulfilled existence.

LIGHTEN THE LOAD WITH YOUR REVIEW

Share the Gift of Lightness

Helping others is the way we help ourselves.

— OPRAH WINFREY

Imagine walking through life with a backpack full of rocks. Each rock is a memory of stress or trauma – a harsh word, a loss, a broken dream. These rocks make it hard to see the beauty in the world, to move freely, and to breathe deeply. But what if I told you that you could set that backpack down? That you don't have to carry that weight alone?

That's the heart of Somatic Therapy 101: Interactive Guide to Alleviate Stress, Overcome Deep-Rooted Trauma, and Strengthen the Mind-Body Connection with Easy Tools and Exercises. This book isn't just about understanding the rocks in your backpack; it's about learning how to take them out, one by one, and leave them behind.

So many of us walk around carrying these invisible burdens. In fact, it's said that 70% of adults have faced a traumatic event at least once in their lives. That's a lot of heavy backpacks. But the journey of healing and lightness isn't just for us; it's for everyone who feels weighed down by their past.

This is where you come in. Your experience with this book could be a beacon of hope for someone still struggling to find their way. By sharing your review, you're not just offering your thoughts; you're extending a hand to someone who needs it.

Would you be willing to share your journey to help another?

It doesn't cost anything but a moment of your time. Yet, your words could be the nudge someone needs to start their own process of healing. Your review could help...

...one more person feel a little lighter. ...one more soul find peace. ...one more heart rediscover joy. ...one more mind connect deeply with their body. ...one more life change for the better.

All it takes is a few clicks to leave your review:

Simply scan the QR code below or visit this link:

https://www.amazon.com/review/create-review/?
asin=B0D2NNZPGM

If you're moved by the idea of helping someone step into a lighter, freer version of themselves, then you're exactly who this book was written for. Welcome to a community of healers and learners, all dedicated to helping each other grow.

I'm so excited to continue this journey with you, exploring even more ways to connect with ourselves and the world around us without the weight of our pasts.

Thank you from the deepest part of my heart for your willingness to share your experience. Together, we can make a world of difference, one review at a time.

- Your guide and fellow traveler, Lizanne Douglas

P.S. - Sharing is one of the most powerful tools we have for connection and healing. If this book has helped you, consider passing it along to someone else who might be carrying their own backpack of rocks. Your recommendation could be the first step towards their journey of healing and lightness.

CHAPTER SIX

SOMATIC THERAPY AS AN ALTERNATIVE PATH

Have you ever felt like traditional talk therapy stalled out before reaching the heart of your pain? This chapter addresses the untapped possibilities of somatic therapy that go beyond words—penetrating the depths of your being.

EXPLORING SOMATIC THERAPY IN VARIOUS LIFE STAGES AND SITUATIONS

Somatic therapy offers a personalized approach to help you navigate the unique challenges you face throughout life. It equips you with tools to manage stress, transition through life's changes, and adapt to physical limitations, all through practices that deepen your connection with your body.

As you encounter transitional anxieties, whether from life changes, career shifts, or personal growth, somatic therapy acts as a stabilizing force. It encourages you to tune into your body's signals, creating a space where anxieties can be acknowledged and managed. This practice aims to balance your nervous system, guiding you gently through periods of uncertainty with increased resilience.

Somatic therapy, with its versatile and effective approach, emphasizes listening to your body's wisdom. This journey invites you to explore a path of well-being that is both profound and personal, helping you face life's challenges with grace and awareness.

Somatic Therapy across Life Stages

Somatic therapy's flexibility and efficacy shine when tailored to meet the distinct challenges encountered at different stages of life. Each period brings its own set of stressors and anxieties, and somatic therapy offers unique tools and techniques to address these, facilitating growth, healing, and well-being.

Young Adulthood

During young adulthood, individuals often face the dual pressures of establishing their identity and navigating the complexities of adult life. This period can be fraught with trauma and high stress, particularly as young adults make significant life transitions—entering college, starting careers, or forming deep relationships. Somatic therapy plays a crucial role here, utilizing mind-body techniques to release stress and trauma "locked away" in the body. Techniques such as grounding exercises, breathwork, and guided movement help young adults learn to self-regulate their emotions and physiological responses, providing a foundation for healing deep-seated trauma with the support of a mental health professional. For those dealing with post-traumatic stress disorder (PTSD), somatic therapy's emphasis on bodily awareness and connection offers a path to address and mitigate symptoms, fostering resilience and empowerment.

Midlife

Midlife brings its own unique challenges, often characterized by transitional anxieties, relationship tensions, and questions of purpose and fulfillment. The increased external demands and uncertainties of this life stage can lead to significant stress and anxiety. Somatic therapy addresses these challenges by focusing on regulating the nervous system and fostering a balance between its sympathetic and parasympathetic branches. Through somatic resources such as mindful breath, intentional movement, and body awareness practices, individuals can navigate midlife transitions more gracefully. These techniques offer immediate relief from anxiety and serve as long-term strategies for maintaining emotional and physiological balance, helping individuals to stay connected to their sense of self and navigate the complexities of midlife with confidence and clarity.

Older Age

As individuals enter older age, they often confront physical limitations and somatic symptom disorders (SSDs), which can significantly impact their quality of life and well-being. Somatic therapy, in conjunction with approaches like cognitive behavioral therapy (CBT), has shown promise in addressing SSDs, including reducing pain intensity and disability. This therapy is particularly beneficial for managing chronic pain, a prevalent issue among older adults. By focusing on gentle, adaptive exercises and practices that respect the body's current capabilities, somatic therapy helps to alleviate discomfort, enhance mobility, and improve overall well-being. Furthermore, it addresses the emotional and psychological aspects of aging, offering older adults strategies to cope with physical changes and maintain a positive, engaged approach to life.

Integrating Somatic Therapy with Other Modalities

Integrating somatic therapy with different therapeutic techniques offers a comprehensive approach to healing that transcends the limitations of any single therapeutic practice. By combining somatic therapy with other healing modalities, such as psychotherapy, meditation, physical exercises, Gestalt therapy, and object relations theory, individuals can experience a more holistic path to wellness that addresses the complexity of the human experience.

Complementing Psychotherapy

Somatic therapy enhances traditional psychotherapy by adding a bodily dimension to the exploration of thoughts and emotions. Where psychotherapy might focus on cognitive and emotional understanding, somatic therapy brings awareness to how these cognitive processes and emotional states are experienced in the body. This integration allows for a more profound healing process, as individuals learn not only to understand their experiences but also to feel and process them through their bodies. Techniques like breathwork, posture adjustment, and mindful movement can be incorporated into psychotherapy sessions, providing clients with tools to directly engage with and process their emotions.

Enhancing Meditation Practices

Meditation and mindfulness practices benefit significantly from the incorporation of somatic elements. Somatic therapy teaches individuals to notice and interpret the subtle cues their bodies send, which can deepen the meditative experience. By bringing a somatic approach to mindfulness, individuals can explore a more embodied form of meditation, often referred to as somatic meditation. This practice encourages a deeper connection with bodily sensations, promoting a state of presence and groundedness that complements the mental and emotional focuses of traditional meditation practices.

Physical Exercises

Physical exercises, when integrated with somatic therapy, can be tailored to not just enhance physical fitness but also to support emotional and psychological well-being. Somatic therapy provides a framework for understanding how movement affects emotional states, allowing for the development of exercise routines that specifically aim to release tension, reduce stress, and improve mood. Practices such as yoga, tai chi, and qigong, which inherently combine movement with mindful awareness, align closely with somatic principles, offering a seamless blend of physical activity and therapeutic self-exploration.

Integration with Gestalt Therapy and Focusing

Gestalt therapy's emphasis on awareness, present-moment experience, and the therapeutic relationship finds a powerful complement in somatic therapy. The integration of somatic practices allows Gestalt therapists to work with clients on a more visceral level, exploring not just their thoughts and feelings but also how these are manifested in the body. Similarly, the focusing technique, which involves paying close attention to internal bodily experiences, naturally aligns with somatic therapy, enhancing the process of gaining insight and achieving psychological change.

Relational Somatic Psychotherapy

Relational somatic psychotherapy expands on the principles of somatic therapy by emphasizing the role of the therapeutic relationship and interpersonal dynamics in the healing process. This modality integrates somatic awareness with relational techniques, helping individuals understand how their bodily experiences influence and are influenced by their relationships. It offers a pathway to explore how early relationships are internalized and manifested within the body, drawing on insights from object relations theory to deepen the therapeutic work.

Object Relations Theory

Object relations theory, which focuses on how early relationships with caregivers are internalized and shape one's interactions and experiences, can be enriched by somatic therapy. By integrating somatic practices, therapists can help clients not only to cognitively understand these early relational patterns but also to embody and work through them. Somatic therapy offers a means to access and heal these deep-seated wounds, facilitating a process of transformation that is both psychological and physical.

The Containment with Safe Touch Technique

The containment with safe touch technique involves using gentle self-touch to create a sense of safety and containment. For individuals experiencing anxiety or feeling overwhelmed, placing hands over the heart or wrapping arms around oneself can provide immediate comfort and grounding. This practice can be integrated into daily routines or used in moments of distress to foster a sense of security.

Pendulation

Pendulation refers to the movement between states of tension and relaxation, helping the body recognize its capacity to return to a state of balance. This technique is particularly useful for individuals dealing with trauma. By gently focusing on an area of discomfort and then shifting attention to a neutral or pleasant sensation elsewhere in the body, individuals learn to navigate and alleviate distress.

Rhythmic Movement

Incorporating the rhythmic movement technique, such as gentle rocking or swaying, can soothe the nervous system and reduce stress levels. This approach draws on the body's natural rhythms to foster relaxation and emotional balance. Rhythmic movement can be especially beneficial in addressing insomnia, anxiety, and hyperarousal states.

Bioenergetics

Bioenergetics exercises focus on releasing chronic muscle tension and freeing restricted breathing patterns. Techniques may include grounding exercises, stretches, and movements that promote energetic flow throughout the body. Bioenergetics is effective in addressing emotional issues rooted in bodily tension and can enhance overall vitality and well-being.

Self-Regulation Techniques

Self-regulation techniques empower individuals to manage their physiological and emotional responses. Practices such as focused breathing, mindfulness, and guided imagery help individuals cultivate a deep sense of inner calm and resilience against stressors.

The Voo Sound

Using the voo sound entails making the "voo" sound on long exhales. It's a powerful way to engage the vagus nerve, which plays a critical role in regulating the body's relaxation response. This simple vocal exercise can be used to calm the nervous system, reduce anxiety, and promote a sense of inner peace.

It always beneficial to learn and practice these techniques under the guidance of a trained professional, especially when working through trauma.

7-Step Somatic Exercise to Process Triggers

Step 1: Notice Bodily Distress

Begin by identifying where in your body you feel distress, such as tightness in your stomach or clenched fists.

Step 2: Deep Breathing

Take ten deep breaths, focusing on elongating the exhale to activate the body's relaxation response.

Step 3: Safe Space Visualization

Recall a place where you feel completely safe and at ease. Vividly imagine this space, using all your senses to immerse yourself fully.

Step 4: Instinctive Movement

Allow your body to move in ways that feel instinctively comforting—shaking, swaying, or stomping can help release pent-up energy.

Step 5: Focus on Your Anchor

Return your attention to your safe space visualization, using it as an anchor to ground yourself.

Step 6: Make the "Voo" Sound

Use long exhales to vocalize the "voo" sound, helping to calm your nervous system further.

Step 7: Loving Words of Comfort

Offer yourself kind, comforting words—what you need to hear in the moment to feel supported and understood.

Personal Stories of Transformation

In the stories below, you will be able to see how integrated somatic therapy can dig deep to go where traditional therapy falls short.

Gabby's Healing Path

Gabby Bernstein, celebrated motivational speaker and author, opens up about her intimate journey toward healing in her book *Happy Days: The Guided Path from Trauma to Profound Freedom and Inner Peace.*

Gabby's exploration into the realm of somatic experiences began after an unexpected moment of paralysis during a light-hearted race with her husband—she found herself inexplicably unable to run. This puzzling physical response prompted her to delve deeper into understanding her body's reaction through Somatic Experiencing therapy.

Through SE therapy, Gabby embarked on a profound journey to untangle and liberate her body from the grips of trauma. The process involved gently guiding her awareness of bodily sensations and responses, allowing her to process and release trauma stored within her body. This approach helped her to reconnect with her physical self in a deeply healing way, paving a path toward profound freedom and inner peace.

Gabby's story is a testament to the transformative power of somatic experiences. It highlights how, by tuning into our body's wisdom and embracing the healing potential of SE therapy, we can overcome the barriers that trauma erects in our lives. Her journey serves as an inspiring example of how somatic practices can lead us to discover a more liberated and peaceful existence.

Daniella's Somatic Experiencing Journey

Daniella, a dedicated professional always seeking to deepen her understanding and skills, embarked on a journey into Somatic experiencing by attending specialized training. The experience was transformative for her, opening up new pathways of connection and understanding both in her professional practice and her personal life.

Through the SE training, Daniella learned to approach her work with a more grounded presence, integrating the principles of somatic therapy to foster a safe and healing environment for those she worked with. The training taught her to tune into the subtle cues of the body, recognizing how trauma and stress manifest physically and how to guide others in releasing these deeply held patterns.

However, the impact of the SE training went beyond her professional practice. Daniella found herself applying these principles to her own life, cultivating a more compassionate relationship with herself. She learned to listen to her body's needs, to honor its wisdom, and to approach her own experiences and emotions with the same gentleness and respect she offered her clients.

This newfound approach also transformed her relationships with others. Daniella became more attuned to the nonverbal cues of those around her, enabling her to respond with greater empathy and understanding. Her interactions became more meaningful, and her connections became deeper as she applied the somatic principles of presence, grounding, and compassion in her daily life.

Daniella's journey through SE training was not just an educational experience but a deeply moving journey that enriched her professional skills and personal growth. It allowed her to develop a more holistic approach to healing, one that embraces the inter-connectedness of mind, body, and spirit in fostering well-being and peace.

INTERACTIVE ELEMENT

I would like to invite you to put what you've learned above into action by completing the following:

Somatic Therapy Goal-Setting Worksheet

Embarking on a journey with somatic therapy requires clarity and intention. This detailed worksheet is designed to help you articulate and plan for both your immediate and far-reaching goals within the realm of somatic therapy. Whether you aim to enhance your physical flexibility, alleviate stress, or heal from past traumas, setting clear goals is a critical first step.

Part 1: Identifying Your Goals

1. Reflection:

Begin with a moment of reflection. Consider the aspects of your life you wish to transform through somatic therapy. Think about how your body feels daily, moments when you experience discomfort, and what you imagine your life would be like without these barriers.

2. Goal Articulation:

Short-term Goals: Identify goals you hope to achieve in the coming weeks or months. These should be specific, measurable, and achievable objectives that will lead to immediate improvements in your well-being.

Example: "I want to reduce my stress levels after work through 15 minutes of daily somatic breathing exercises."

Long-term Goals: Consider what you wish to achieve in the year ahead or beyond. Long-term goals often involve deeper, more profound changes.

Example: "I aim to heal from the trauma of a past accident, recognizing and releasing the tension it has caused in my body."

Part 2: Action Steps

For each goal listed, outline specific steps you plan to take to achieve them. This might include daily practices, sessions with a somatic therapist, or educational resources you intend to explore.

Short-term Goals:

Step 1: Research and learn three somatic breathing techniques by [date].
Step 2: Practice the identified techniques each evening after work.
Step 3: Journal any changes in stress levels weekly to monitor progress.

Long-term Goals:

Step 1: Schedule an initial consultation with a certified somatic therapist by [date].
Step 2: Commit to biweekly therapy sessions for a minimum of six months.
Step 3: Participate in a somatic therapy workshop or group session focused on trauma recovery.

Part 3: Resources and Support

Short-term Goal Resources:

- A list of recommended somatic therapy exercises and techniques.
- Access to online forums where individuals share their experiences and advice.

Long-term Goal Resources:

- Recommended reading on healing from trauma through somatic therapy.
- Contact information for local somatic therapy practitioners and support groups.

Part 4: Monitoring Progress

Create a system for tracking your progress toward each goal. This could involve regular check-ins with yourself, updating a journal, or sharing updates with a support group or therapist.

Weekly Check-Ins: Set aside time each week to reflect on your progress, any challenges you've encountered, and adjustments needed to stay on track.

FINAL THOUGHTS

In this chapter, we've explored the profound potential of somatic therapy as an alternative path to healing, delving into its application across various life stages and situations. From addressing the stress and trauma often encountered in young adulthood to navigating the transitional anxieties of midlife and confronting the physical limitations of older age, somatic therapy offers personalized tools and techniques to foster growth, healing, and well-being. We've seen how somatic therapy's adaptability makes it an invaluable resource for managing life's challenges, emphasizing the importance of tuning into our body's wisdom.

As you reflect on the insights and examples shared, consider how somatic therapy might enrich your own journey toward healing and self-discovery. Whether you're seeking to reduce stress, improve flexibility, or heal from past trauma, the practices outlined here provide a foundation for integrating mind-body awareness into your approach to wellness.

Looking ahead, with our newfound understanding of somatic therapy's versatility and effectiveness, we're poised to take the next step: putting theory into practice. The upcoming chapter will guide you through incorporating somatic exercises into your daily life and transforming theoretical knowledge into practical, healing actions. Get ready to learn how to weave somatic practices into your everyday routines, enabling a continuous journey of self-awareness, healing, and growth. Stay tuned for actionable strategies that will help you embody the principles of somatic therapy, making every day an opportunity for profound personal transformation.

CHAPTER SEVEN

DAILY PRACTICES FOR SOMATIC WELLNESS

P icture this: Your day begins with a sense of calm that stays with you until you turn off the lights at night. Life's curve-balls? You handle them with ease. This can be your everyday reality with a routine of somatic practices designed for real life.

MICHELLE'S MORNING ROUTINE MIRACLE

Michelle had always been the type to hit the snooze button, and in her mornings, there was a blur of missed alarms and rushed coffee. But as the stress of her job began to creep into her evenings, staining them with the same hectic energy, she knew something had to change. She stumbled upon the concept of a daily somatic routine, a practice that promised equilibrium amid chaos.

With diligence, Michelle crafted her morning and evening rituals. Mornings began with a series of stretches and breathing exercises, each movement a silent conversation with her body, acknowl-edging any tightness or discomfort and inviting in calm and focus. Evenings ended with mindfulness meditation, a practice that helped her shed the weight of the day's worries. This was not a one-size-fits-all solution; Michelle adapted her routines to fit into her life's varying rhythms, some days finding only brief moments for reflection, other days immersing herself in longer sessions of self-care.

The change was gradual, like the slow opening of a bloom. Her colleagues began to notice a steadier pace in her step and a more present gaze during conversations. Michelle found herself navigating deadlines with a newfound poise and facing challenges with a composed heart. Her routines had become her anchor, a steadfast presence that allowed her to move through her days with a sense of peace that was once just a wistful sigh in the morning rush.

Embarking on Your Own Somatic Journey

As you pursue your own holistic wellness through somatic practices, you'll find it's a transformative approach that emphasizes internal physical perception and experience. It's a path woven with the threads of mindfulness and physicality, leading to a harmonious balance between the two. Imagine starting each day with an intention not just to live but to thrive, with your body as your guide.

Morning: Awakening with Intention

As dawn breaks and the world slowly comes to life, carve out a sanctuary of time for yourself. In the stillness of the morning, you might consider lying down and conducting a mindful check-in from head to toe, tuning into the subtle sensations that often go unnoticed.

Visualize the tailbone as a gentle paintbrush, guiding the flow of movements across the canvas of your morning. With each arch and curl of the spine, connect with the rhythm of your breath and the contraction and elongation of your muscles. This practice is not just a physical warm-up; it's a ritual that helps reclaim autonomy over your muscles, eases stiffness, and prepares you for the day with renewed control and poise.

Daytime: Sustaining Momentum

Throughout the day, maintain a connection to your body's dialogue. Integrate somatic practices into your daily activities. Take moments—even if just a minute or two here and there—to reconnect, using breath as an anchor to return to a state of internal awareness. This ongoing practice can be your secret to maintaining emotional balance and managing stress as the day progresses.

Evening: Unwinding into Tranquility

When night falls, consider transitioning to practices that focus on decompression and release. Engage in movements that allow for the shedding of the day's pressures. Embrace poses and stretches that facilitate relaxation and prepare you for restorative sleep.

Adapting Your Practice to Different Time Constraints And Energy Levels

Recognize that life's demands fluctuate, and your somatic practice should flexibly respond to these changes. On days filled with abundant time, a more extended session might be possible. When time is limited or energy is low, consider scaling back. A brief 10-minute session can still be incredibly effective. Modify the movements, simplify the routine, or opt for no movements at all to fit your current state.

Find a rhythm that fits seamlessly into your daily life, making this practice a regular part of your routine. It's less about adhering to a strict schedule and more about creating a dependable rhythm for your body and mind.

Over time, the commitment to somatic practice starts to manifest its benefits in your life. You may begin to notice a shift—a newfound calmness in the face of challenges, increased resilience to stress, and a rejuvenated sense of movement. Your body becomes an instrument and a composer of well-being, orchestrating a symphony that resonates with your daily life's rhythm.

As you continue on this path, the practice evolves with you. It's a relationship built on trust and attentive listening, where the body leads, and you follow with grace. This isn't just about experiencing tranquility during the quiet moments of dawn or dusk; it's about cultivating that tranquility to carry with you throughout the day's peaks and valleys.

Consider this somatic dance, where you are both the dancer and the dance, navigating life with an embodied awareness that turns every motion into self-care and every breath into a moment of profound connection. This is the essence of the somatic way—a path of presence, a life embraced with depth and intention, a journey into the very core of your being.

Exercises for Everyday Practice

By incorporating these somatic exercises into your daily routine, you can enhance mindfulness, reduce stress, and improve your physical wellness through gentle and deliberate movements. Each exercise is designed to foster a deeper connection with your body, allowing for a harmonious balance between mind and physical well-being.

Somatic Breathing Exercises

Diaphragmatic Breathing: Begin by finding a comfortable seated or lying position. Place one hand on your chest and the other on your abdomen. Inhale deeply through the nose, aiming to make the hand on your abdomen rise higher than the one on your chest. This encourages full engagement of the diaphragm. Exhale slowly through the mouth, focusing on a complete release of breath.

Extended Exhalation: Practice inhaling for a count of four, then extend your exhale to a count of eight. This exercise aids in activating the body's relaxation response, reducing stress, and promoting a calm mind.

Gentle Stretches

Neck Release: Gently tilt your head toward one shoulder, feeling a stretch on the opposite side of your neck. Hold this position for a few breaths, then switch sides. This movement is beneficial for relieving neck tension and improving mobility.

Seated Torso Circles: While seated, place your hands on your knees and initiate small circles with your torso, moving from the hips. Circle in one direction for several rotations before switching. This helps to loosen the lower back and increase fluidity in the torso's movements.

Mindful Movements

Seated Cat-Cow: Position yourself at the edge of a chair with your feet firmly on the ground. With hands on your knees, arch your back and look upward as you inhale (Cow Pose), and round your spine, bringing your chin to your chest as you exhale (Cat Pose). This sequence encourages flexibility and circulation in the spine.

Supine Spinal Twist: Lying on your back, bring your knees to your chest and then gently lower them to one side while turning your head to the opposite direction. This twist is excellent for relieving tension in the spine and promoting relaxation.

Somatic Stretching Exercises

Embryo Pose or Child's Pose: From a kneeling position, sit back on your heels and fold forward, extending your arms. This posture helps release tension from the back and shoulders and offers a moment of introspection and calm.

Bridge Pose: Lying on your back with knees bent, press into your feet to lift your hips, aiming to create a straight line from your shoulders to your knees. This strengthens the back and enhances spinal flexibility.

Waterfall: Lie with your back on the floor and elevate your legs up against a wall. This inversion aids in reducing swelling in the legs and can relax the muscles of the lower back.

Legs-Up-the-Chair Pose: Similar to waterfall, but more accessible for some, sit close to a chair and lie back, placing your lower legs on the seat of the chair. This variant provides gentle relief for the back and legs and can be especially soothing for the lower back.

Pigeon Pose: From a hands-and-knees position, bring one knee forward toward your hand and let the opposite leg extend back, resting on the floor. This pose deeply stretches the hip rotators and flexors, which is beneficial for those who sit for long periods of time.

Thread the Needle Pose: While on all fours, slide one arm under the body with the palm facing up, and lower your shoulder to the floor, extending the other arm in front of you or wrapping it around your back. This pose offers a gentle twist and stretch to the shoulders and upper back.

Seated Forward Bend: Sitting with legs extended forward, hinge at the hips to lean forward, reaching for your feet or shins. This stretch targets the hamstrings and lower back, promoting flexibility and relieving tension.

Tailoring Routines to Your Physical and Emotional Needs

Tailoring somatic routines to individual needs is a crucial aspect of integrating these practices effectively into one's life. Here's a detailed exploration of how to personalize somatic routines, emphasizing the importance of customization, methods for assessing specific needs, and suggestions for adapting routines to various lifestyles.

Importance of Personalization

Customizing somatic practices is essential because it acknowledges the unique physical, emotional, and circumstantial factors influencing each individual. This personalization ensures that the practices are more effective, directly addressing the individual's areas of tension, discomfort, or imbalance. By focusing on personal goals and preferences, individuals can engage in practices that not only offer relief but also contribute to long-term wellness and resilience.

Assessing Specific Needs

Creating an effective somatic routine begins with a comprehensive assessment of one's current physical and emotional state, as well as personal wellness goals.

Physical and Emotional Well-Being: As you participate in exercises, your needs and capabilities may change. Be sure to assess yourself periodically to adjust to any changes, emotionally or physically.

Personal Goals: Define what you aim to achieve through your somatic practice. Whether it's reducing stress, enhancing flexibility, or fostering a deeper sense of peace, understanding your objectives will guide your choice of practices.

Experimentation: Explore a variety of somatic practices to discover which ones align with your needs and preferences. This exploration is key to building a routine that feels rewarding and sustainable.

Modifying Routines for Various Lifestyles

Adapting somatic practices to fit different lifestyles ensures that everyone can enjoy the benefits of these practices, regardless of their daily commitments or challenges.

For Busy Professionals: Incorporate brief, targeted sessions into the workday. Short mindfulness exercises or quick stretching breaks can significantly impact stress levels and focus.

For Parents: Practice somatic exercises with your children, turning it into an opportunity for learning and bonding. Activities like family yoga can be both fun and beneficial, setting a foundation for healthy habits early on.

Adapting to Time and Energy: Be mindful of your energy levels and time constraints, adjusting the intensity and duration of your practices accordingly. This flexibility will help maintain consistency in your routine without causing additional stress or fatigue.

Integration into Daily Activities: Find ways to integrate somatic practices into routine activities. Mindful breathing during your commute or body awareness while doing chores can seamlessly incorporate these practices into your life, making them more accessible and less time-consuming.

INTERACTIVE ELEMENT

I would like to invite you to create a **Personal Somatic Routine Planner**—a pivotal step toward fostering a deeper connection with yourself through somatic practices. This planner is designed to be a dynamic tool that adapts to the rhythms of your daily life, addressing your unique needs, preferences, and the challenges you face. Here's how to create and utilize a personalized planner:

Identifying Your Needs and Preferences

Start by taking a moment to reflect on what you aim to achieve with your somatic practices. Are you looking to reduce stress, enhance physical flexibility, or cultivate mental clarity? Understanding your goals is crucial. Next, assess your current physical and emotional state. Where do you hold tension? What emotional challenges are you navigating? This self-reflection will guide the customization of your planner.

Structuring Your Day

Consider the natural flow of your day. Are mornings rushed, or do you have a quiet start? What does your energy level look like in the evening? Use this insight to allocate specific times for your somatic practices. You might find that a gentle, energizing routine suits your morning, while a calming, grounding practice is perfect for unwinding in the evening.

Selecting Your Practices

With a clear understanding of your needs and daily rhythm, choose somatic exercises that align with your goals. Incorporate a mix of breathing techniques, gentle stretches, and mindful movements. For instance, start your day with diaphragmatic breathing to activate your parasympathetic nervous system, promoting relaxation and focus. In the evening, engage in a sequence of gentle yoga poses to release physical and mental tension.

Adapting to Life's Variability

Your planner should have the flexibility to accommodate changes in your schedule and energy levels. Designate shorter, more focused practices for busy days, ensuring you can maintain consistency even when time is scarce. Include options for extending or intensifying your routine on days when you have more time or energy.

Integration into Daily Activities

Look for opportunities to weave somatic awareness into your everyday activities. This might mean practicing mindful breathing while commuting or performing a series of discreet stretches during your lunch break. The goal is to keep the principles of somatic practice alive throughout your day, enhancing your connection to the present moment and your physical self.

Reflective Practice

Include a section in your planner for reflection. At the end of each day or week, jot down notes about what worked well, what challenges you encountered, and any adjustments you want to make. This reflective practice ensures your routine continues to evolve with you, remaining aligned with your changing needs and preferences.

Implementing Your Planner

Once you've outlined your personalized somatic routine planner, the next step is implementation. You might choose to create a digital planner using tools for easy adjustments and reminders, or you might prefer a physical journal for a tactile, unplugged experience. Regardless of the format, the key to success lies in regular engagement with your planner, allowing it to serve as a living document that guides your somatic journey.

You can use this template or any other template that suits your needs. Templatelab.com has free templates you can access and customize as needed.

PERSONAL SOMATIC **PLANNER**   Date: _____

APPOINTMENTS

05:00 _____
05:30 _____
06:00 _____
06:30 _____
07:00 _____
07:30 _____
08:00 _____
08:30 _____
09:00 _____
09:30 _____
10:00 _____
10:30 _____
11:00 _____
11:30 _____
12:00 _____
12:30 _____
13:00 _____
13:30 _____
14:00 _____
14:30 _____
15:00 _____
15:30 _____
16:00 _____
16:30 _____
17:00 _____
17:30 _____
18:00 _____
18:30 _____
19:00 _____
19:30 _____
20:00 _____
20:30 _____
21:00 _____
21:30 _____
22:00 _____
22:30 _____
23:00 _____
23:30 _____
24:00 _____

GOALS FOR THE DAY

REMINDER

○ _____
○ _____
○ _____
○ _____
○ _____
○ _____
○ _____
○ _____

DAILY ACTIVITIES

I'M GRATEFUL FOR

NOTES

TemplateLAB

FINAL THOUGHTS

In this chapter, you explored the profound impact of somatic practices on personal development and wellness, diving even deeper into covering the importance of the holistic connection between your body and mind, highlighting the significance of mindfulness, movement, and breathwork as tools to enhance self-awareness.

You discovered the importance of weaving somatic exercises into your daily routine to boost mindfulness, balance emotions, and improve physical health. The chapter illustrated that with dedicated and consistent practice, you can achieve a harmonious alignment between your physical and emotional states, leading to a more fulfilling and centered life.

You were encouraged to embrace these practices with an open heart and curiosity, promising that this journey would be both enriching and transformative, and were provided a template to help you integrate these techniques into your life. By applying these methods, you can now unlock significant benefits for your well-being.

Looking ahead, the next chapter promises to expand on these foundations. You'll delve into strategies for sustaining and deepening your somatic practices over time, transforming them into a lifelong pursuit of self-discovery and wellness. Expect to learn how to embed these practices more deeply into your life, ensuring they continue to enrich your journey toward personal growth and well-being.

CHAPTER EIGHT

EMBRACING THE SOMATIC JOURNEY

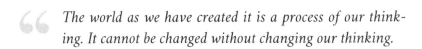

The world as we have created it is a process of our think-
ing. It cannot be changed without changing our thinking.

— ALBERT EINSTEIN

A s you have learned, incorporating somatic practices into your daily life offers a comprehensive pathway to enhanced well-being, emphasizing the importance of a holistic health approach that encompasses both mind and body. Rooted in the principle of somatic awareness, these practices present long-term advantages for stress management, emotional stability, and overall health improvement. They empower you to develop a deeper connection with your bodily sensations and emotions, fostering a profound understanding of yourself and paving the way for mental clarity, emotional resilience, and a harmonious balance between your physical and emotional states.

INCORPORATING LONG-TERM SOMATIC PRACTICES INTO YOUR SCHEDULE

In the fast-paced, stress-filled modern environment, adopting long-term somatic strategies is essential for nurturing balance and wellness. Practices such as mindfulness, meditation, yoga, and body-awareness exercises underscore the vital link between mind and body when implemented over time. This connection not only deepens self-awareness but also provides a sustainable path to enhance your well-being.

The cornerstone of these practices is their capacity to modulate the body's stress response. By focusing on the present and tuning into your body's cues, you can interrupt the cycle of chronic stress and mitigate its detrimental health effects. Engaging regularly in somatic practices leads to notable benefits, including reduced symptoms of anxiety and depression, lowered blood pressure, and improved sleep quality, all of which contribute to a healthier, more balanced life.

These practices equip you with a toolkit for navigating daily stressors and boosting emotional regulation. Cultivating mindfulness and body awareness allows you to detect early signs of stress and apply techniques to diminish its impact, such as using deep breathing and mindful movement to activate the body's relaxation response.

A holistic health approach advocated by somatic practices emphasizes the interplay between physical activity, nutrition, and mental well-being. This integrated perspective fosters a deeper connection with oneself and the world, enriching life with a sense of purpose and fulfillment.

Embedding somatic practices into your routine can be both simple and accessible. As discussed in previous chapters, you may want to consider starting your day with mindfulness meditation, incorpo-rating brief movement or stretching breaks during work, or engaging in yoga or breathing exercises in the evening. The essence of these practices lies in their consistent and purposeful application.

To seamlessly weave somatic practices into your lifestyle, consider these strategies:

- **Routine and Consistency:** As mentioned previously, dedicate specific times each day for somatic exercises like morning meditation or evening yoga to cultivate a regular practice habit.
- **Variety and Personalization:** Dive into a wide array of somatic practices, as mentioned before, to find those that truly click with you, ensuring your routine stays engaging and addresses various aspects of your well-being.
- **Mindful Integration:** Integrate mindfulness and body awareness into daily activities to enhance the effectiveness and applicability of your practice.
- **Community and Support:** Join classes or groups to gain motivation and a sense of belonging, enriching your experience through shared learning and support.
- **Education and Reflection:** Invest time in learning about somatic theories and techniques and engage in reflective practices to deepen your appreciation and understanding of their benefits.

Will's Willingness to Change

Will, a software developer, found himself constantly caught in the cycle of deadlines and digital demands. Despite his achievements, he felt a persistent sense of stress and disconnection from his own well-being.

One evening, driven by a need for change, Will stumbled upon a group practicing yoga in a quiet corner of his local park. The sight of their calm and focus amid the city's usual noise intrigued him. After the session, he chatted with the instructor, who introduced him to the concept of somatic practices and their role in fostering a mind-body connection for improved health and balance.

Motivated by this encounter, Will decided to explore these practices further. He started with mindfulness meditation each morning, setting aside a few minutes to sit in silence and observe his breath. This small change began to make a noticeable difference in his daily routine, offering him moments of calm before diving into work.

Encouraged by this initial success, Will integrated short yoga sessions into his evenings. These practices helped him unwind from the day's stress, stretching away the physical tension built up from hours at his desk and clearing his mind before bedtime.

Over time, Will noticed significant improvements in his life. His concentration sharpened, making him more efficient at work without feeling constantly overwhelmed. His sleep quality improved, allowing him to wake up feeling refreshed and ready for the day. He became more aware of his stress triggers and learned to manage them through deep breathing and mindful pauses throughout his day.

Will's journey didn't stop at personal benefits. His more balanced approach to life positively affected his relationships. He became more present and attentive in conversations, fostering deeper connections with friends and family.

A year after discovering somatic practices, Will shared his experience with others feeling the weight of similar stresses. He emphasized the value of starting small, finding practices that fit one's lifestyle, and the importance of consistency. Through mindfulness and yoga, Will found not just relief from stress but also a deeper connection to himself and a more fulfilling life.

His story underscores the accessible and transformative power of somatic practices when used in a long-term strategy, showing how they can be a vital tool for anyone looking to navigate life's demands with greater ease and resilience.

ADVANCED WELLNESS

To deepen the integration of somatic practices into your lifestyle and to explore the growth and healing potential these practices offer over time, let's focus on actionable steps and the transformative impact of continued engagement with somatic methods. Building upon the foundational practices previously mentioned, here are detailed exercises and an explanation of how sustained practice can foster deeper self-awareness and healing:

Dynamic Earth Connection

Step 1: Find Your Base

Stand with your feet shoulder-width apart, knees slightly bent. Allow your arms to hang loosely at your sides.

Step 2: Begin to Sway

Gently sway your body from side to side, forward and backward, feeling the support of the earth beneath your feet.

Step 3: Integrate Arm Movements

Slowly raise your arms, letting them move fluidly as if energy were flowing from the earth through your feet, up your body, and out through your fingertips. Move your arms in natural, flowing motions that feel good to you.

Step 4: Incorporate Head and Neck Movements

Gently turn your head from side to side, aligning your neck movements with the swaying of your body and arms, enhancing the feeling of flow and connection.

Step 5: Ground Yourself

Gradually slow your movements, coming to a standstill. Take a few deep breaths, feeling a deep sense of grounding and connection to the earth.

Sensory Awakening

Step 1: Settle into Stillness

Sit or lie down in a comfortable position. Close your eyes and take a few deep breaths to center yourself.

Step 2: Engage Your Senses Sequentially

- **Sound:** Focus on the sounds around you, near and far. Notice them without judgment.
- **Touch**: Feel the air on your skin, the weight of your body on the chair or floor.
- **Smell:** Notice any aromas in your environment, letting them come to you naturally.

Step 3: Body Scan with Breath

Start at your toes and slowly move your awareness up through your body, imagining breathing into each part as you go. Notice any sensations without trying to change them.

Step 4: Integration

After reaching the top of your head, take a moment to appreciate the fullness of your sensory experience and the relaxation it brings.

Fluidity and Grace

Step 1: Warm Up with Isolated Movements

Begin by focusing on one body part at a time (e.g., wrists, shoulders, hips) and moving each part gently, exploring its range of motion.

Step 2: Let the Music Guide You

Play music that resonates with your current mood. Let it inspire your movements, starting with small gestures and evolving into full-body expressions.

Step 3: Explore Space and Movement

Move through the space around you, experimenting with different speeds, levels, and dynamics. Allow your body to express itself freely, without judgment.

Step 4: Wind Down

Gradually slow your movements, ending with gentle stretching. Focus on the sensation of stretch and release, embodying the fluidity you've explored.

Integrative Sensory Practice

Step 1: Choose Your Natural Setting

Find a comfortable spot in nature, whether it's a garden, park, or forest.

Step 2: Engage Each Sense

- **Sight**: Observe your surroundings, noticing colors, patterns, and movements.
- **Hearing**: Close your eyes and focus on the natural sounds around you. Try to identify different sources.
- **Smell:** Take deep breaths, inhaling the scents of nature.
- **Touch:** Touch the ground, plants, or a tree. Notice the textures.
- **Taste:** If you've brought a natural snack, eat it slowly, savoring the flavors and textures.

Step 3: Reflect and Connect

After engaging all your senses, sit quietly, reflecting on the experience. Feel the connection with the natural world, appreciating its beauty and your place within it.

It's crucial to approach them not merely as tasks to be checked off a list but as integral components of your lifestyle that enhance your connection to your body and the world around you. This holistic approach goes beyond the basic exercises, focusing on a deeper integration of these practices into various aspects of your life.

Mindful Movement Breaks Throughout the Day

The idea of incorporating mindful movement breaks throughout your day as a consistent part of your lifestyle is an invitation to create small islands of awareness and rejuvenation in your routine. These breaks could be as simple as standing up from your desk, stretching your limbs, or engaging in a series of gentle movements like neck rolls or arm stretches. The key is to transition your awareness from the external to the internal, noticing the sensations that arise in your body with each movement. To make this practice more consistent, set reminders at regular intervals on your phone or computer, encouraging you to pause and reconnect with your body.

Transforming Meals into Somatic Experiences

Turning mealtime into a somatic experience elevates eating from a mere necessity to a mindful practice. Begin by creating a serene environment for your meals, free from distractions like electronic devices or reading materials. As you prepare to eat, engage in a brief meditation, focusing on your breath and the act of being present. When you eat, do so slowly and with intention, observing the textures, flavors, and aromas of your food, as well as the sensations within your body as you nourish it. This practice not only enhances your culinary enjoyment but also fosters a deeper connection to the act of eating and its effects on your body.

Dedicating a Specific Time for Practice

Consistency is key in somatic practices, and dedicating a specific time each day for these exercises can help establish a routine. Whether it's first thing in the morning, during a lunch break, or in the evening, find a time that works best for you and stick to it. This dedicated time should be free from interruptions, allowing you to fully immerse yourself in the practice. Begin with a few minutes of stillness, perhaps sitting or lying down comfortably, and conduct a body scan, observing without judgment the sensations that arise. This not only primes your body for further somatic work but also anchors your practice in routine.

Incorporating Diverse Somatic Exercises

The variety of somatic exercises available means that you can choose practices that resonate with your current physical and emotional state. From gentle, mindful movements that focus on breath and alignment to more dynamic exercises that challenge your balance and coordination, the spectrum of somatic exercises offers something for every level of ability and interest. Incorporate a range of exercises into your routine to keep the practice engaging and to explore different aspects of bodily awareness and movement.

Engaging in Somatic Self-Care

Somatic self-care invites you to listen deeply to your body's needs and to respond with compassion and intention. This might mean adjusting your physical activity based on your energy levels, taking time to rest when you feel fatigued, or choosing foods that nourish and satisfy you on multiple levels. It also involves recognizing and honoring your emotional and mental well-being, perhaps through practices like journaling, engaging in creative activities, or seeking social connections that enrich your sense of self and community.

Utilizing Continued Somatic Experiencing Techniques for Stress

Somatic Experiencing, a unique form of somatic therapy, provides a nuanced approach to managing stress and emotional upheaval by focusing on the rewiring of the nervous system. Unlike other somatic therapies that may employ different methods, SE emphasizes tuning into bodily sensations without a set formula.

Techniques such as mindful awareness of breath and physical sensations, or gently grounding oneself, are integral to SE. These methods are designed not merely to down-regulate distress but to foster a more balanced and adaptive nervous system response, specific to the principles of Somatic Experiencing.

Growth and Healing through Somatic Practices

Over time, growth takes place as you become more attuned to the wisdom of your body's signals and build trust in yourself. This mindful approach allows for a compassionate and patient space where healing can occur at the pace your body and mind are ready to handle. As you continue to practice these somatic techniques, you may find a gradual transformation taking place, one where stress is not a roadblock but a pathway to deeper self-awareness and inner strength.

Lifelong Commitment to Mind-Body Harmony

Embracing somatic therapy as a lifelong journey into mind-body harmony offers a transformative path not just for acute healing but for ongoing personal growth and well-being. This perspective shifts the focus from seeking immediate solutions to fostering a deep, sustained connection with oneself. Here are ways to stay motivated and committed to this enriching practice, along with insights from professionals in the field:

Understanding the Value of Somatic Therapy

The foundational step to a lifelong commitment to somatic therapy is recognizing its profound impact. This approach is not merely about alleviating physical discomfort but also about addressing deeper mental health challenges, including PTSD and depression. Understanding that somatic therapy offers a holistic path to healing—integrating the mental, emotional, and physical—can significantly motivate one to delve deeper into the practice. As research and countless personal testimonies reveal, the benefits of somatic therapy extend well beyond immediate symptom relief, offering a pathway to lasting transformation and resilience.

Lifelong Commitment to Regular Practice

Consistency is key to unlocking the full potential of somatic therapy. Regular engagement with somatic exercises and tools not only aids in regulating the nervous system but also reinforces a sense of safety and stability within the body. This practice becomes a reliable resource for navigating life's challenges, enhancing one's ability to remain centered and grounded even in turbulent times.

The Importance of Self-Care and Resourcing

A lifelong commitment to somatic therapy involves cultivating a robust set of internal and external resources. These resources, whether they be supportive relationships, engaging in activities that bring joy, or practicing mindfulness, contribute to a resilient foundation. Remembering and utilizing these resources, especially during challenging moments, can offer immediate relief to the nervous system and foster a deeper sense of coping and well-being.

Cultivating Mindful Awareness

The journey of somatic therapy is deeply intertwined with developing an acute awareness of the body's signals, from muscle tension and shallow breathing to more subtle cues like emotional shifts. This awareness allows for the early recognition and management of stress and trauma responses, enabling one to navigate life's stresses with greater ease and less reactivity.

The Role of Professional Guidance

Engaging with a trained somatic therapist offers invaluable support and direction on this journey. Professional guidance ensures that the practices are tailored to your unique needs and challenges, providing a safe space to explore and heal. Therapists not only offer techniques to manage and process stress and trauma but also accompany you through the deep inner work, making the journey less daunting and more enriching.

Insights from Somatic Therapists

Somatic therapists underscore the importance of viewing this therapy as a continuous journey. They highlight its effectiveness in treating a wide range of mental health issues and its capacity to teach us how to manage stress, regulate emotions, and foster a profound sense of safety and connection.

Therapist Reagan Robinson nailed it when she said, "When we are grounded in our awareness, we can be more present with what we are experiencing in our bodies—in all the spaces that live between our head and our feet."

Embracing somatic therapy as a lifelong journey empowers us to live authentically, fully connected with our inner selves and the world around us, embodying the essence of life as it was meant to be experienced.

INTERACTIVE ELEMENT

Creating a detailed **Somatic Practice Progress Tracker** involves designing a tool that allows individuals to document their journey through somatic practices meticulously. This tracker will serve not only as a log for frequency and duration but also as a reflective space for emotional and physical insights. Here's a step-by-step guide to creating such a tracker:

Designing Your Tracker Layout

Choose a Format: Decide if you prefer a digital spreadsheet (like Excel or Google Sheets) or a physical notebook/journal. Digital formats offer easy editing and can be accessed from multiple devices, while a physical book might provide a more tactile and personal experience.

Layout Design: Create sections for each day of the week, with ample space for logging practices, durations, emotional states, physical sensations, and any other reflections.

Creating Categories for Comprehensive Tracking

Date and Time: Start with the details of your practice, including the date and time of day.

Practice Type: Specify the type of somatic practice (e.g., body scanning, mindful movement, deep breathing exercises).

Duration: Record how long each session lasts to track how much time you're dedicating to your practice.

Frequency: Note how often you engage in somatic practices within a given week.

Detailing Emotional and Physical States

Pre-Practice Check-in: Before starting your practice, jot down your current emotional state and any notable physical sensations.

Post-Practice Reflection: After your session, reflect on any changes in your emotional well-being and physical sensations. Note any shifts, however subtle, toward relaxation, awareness, or discomfort.

Challenges and Successes: Document any difficulties encountered during the practice and any achievements or breakthroughs.

Reflective Notes and Insights

Insights Gained: Use a section to write down any insights about your body-mind connection, patterns you notice over time, or how certain practices affect you differently.

Adaptations and Adjustments: Note any adjustments made to your practice for better alignment with your needs, such as changing the time of day, duration, or type of somatic exercises.

Weekly and Monthly Summaries

Weekly Reflections: At the end of each week, review your entries and summarize your overall progress, patterns, and any new understandings of your somatic experience.

Monthly Overviews: Compile monthly summaries to observe longer-term trends, improvements, challenges, and the evolving relationship with your somatic practices.

Setting Intentions and Goals

Future Practices: Based on your reflections and insights, set intentions or goals for the coming weeks. This could involve deepening certain practices, exploring new somatic exercises, or focusing on specific emotional or physical areas for growth.

Additional Tips

Be Consistent: Try to make entries regularly to maintain a comprehensive record of your journey.

Stay Nonjudgmental: Approach each entry with a nonjudgmental mindset, recognizing that the journey is as important as the destination.

Seek Patterns: Over time, look for patterns in your emotional and physical responses to different practices, which can guide future practice adjustments.

FINAL THOUGHTS

As we close this chapter on embracing the somatic journey, you've been equipped with a wealth of knowledge and practices to deepen your connection with your body and enhance your overall well-being. This path you're embarking on is much more than just a means to heal from past wounds; it's about continuous evolution, growth, and the cultivation of a profound relationship between your mind, body, and the environment around you.

Throughout this chapter, we've explored various techniques and insights designed to enrich your somatic experience. From grounding exercises to mindful movement and from the integration of somatic practices into your daily life to understanding the significance of a lifelong commitment to mind-body harmony, each segment has been carefully curated to support your journey toward a more connected and authentic existence.

The key takeaways from this chapter are clear: somatic practices are not just exercises but a way of living that emphasizes presence, awareness, and the intentional cultivation of well-being. By incorporating these practices into your routine, you're not only enhancing your physical health but also fostering emotional resilience and mental clarity.

Now is the time to put these ideas into action. Begin by incorporating small, manageable practices into your daily routine. Whether it's mindful breathing, a body scan before bed, or integrating movement breaks throughout your day, each step you take is a valuable part of your journey toward holistic health.

As you move forward, remember that this journey is uniquely yours. It's a process of discovery, learning, and adaptation. There will be challenges and setbacks, but also moments of profound insight and joy. Embrace each experience as an opportunity for growth and a deeper connection with yourself.

Looking ahead, the conclusion of this book will weave together all the topics we've explored, offering you a comprehensive understanding and an empowered mindset to maintain a harmonious balance between your mind and body for years to come. We'll revisit key concepts, reflect on the journey, and provide you with the tools to sustain this balance. This final chapter is not just an end but a beginning—the start of your continued exploration and engagement with the somatic practices that resonate with you, guiding you toward a life lived with intention, presence, and authenticity.

Stay curious, open, and committed to this journey. The path of somatic awareness is rich with possibilities and the potential for transformation. Let's move forward together, embracing each step with mindfulness and anticipation for the growth that lies ahead.

CONCLUSION

As you reflect on the transformative journey you've embarked upon through the pages of *Somatic Therapy 101: A Comprehensive Guide to Understanding Effective Ways to Heal the Body from Trauma and Reduce Stress with Easy and Effective Exercises*, your exploration of somatic therapy extends far beyond the mere acquisition of techniques—it's a profound journey of self-discovery, healing, and personal growth.

Throughout this comprehensive guide, you've delved into the intricate landscape of the mind-body connection, uncovering the vast potential of somatic practices to nurture holistic wellness. From foundational principles such as mindfulness, movement, and breathwork to the practical application of techniques like progressive muscle relaxation, deep tissue massage, and trauma-informed yoga, you've gained a lot of valuable information and tools to navigate the complexities of your inner world and foster resilience in the face of life's challenges.

Yet, beyond the acquisition of techniques lies a deeper understanding—a recognition of the innate wisdom that lies within your body and the profound impact that reconnecting with this wisdom can have on your overall well-being. Through somatic practices, you've learned to listen to the subtle cues and sensations of your body, allowing you to cultivate a deeper sense of self-awareness, presence, and authenticity.

You learned that in today's fast-paced, stress-filled world, incorporating long-term somatic practices into your daily life is essential for nurturing balance and wellness. Practices such as mindfulness, meditation, yoga, and body-awareness exercises underscore the vital link between mind and body, providing a sustainable path to enhance your overall well-being.

By dedicating yourself to these practices regularly, you now know you can effectively modulate your body's stress response, interrupting the cycle of chronic stress and mitigating its detrimental health effects. Engaging regularly in somatic practices leads to a multitude of benefits, including reduced symptoms of anxiety and depression, lowered blood pressure, and improved sleep quality.

These practices equip you with a toolkit for navigating daily stressors and boosting emotional regulation. Cultivating mindfulness and body awareness allows you to detect early signs of stress and apply techniques to diminish its impact, such as using deep breathing and mindful movement to activate the body's relaxation response.

Furthermore, the holistic health approach advocated by somatic practices emphasizes the interplay between physical activity, nutrition, and mental well-being. This integrated perspective fosters a deeper connection with yourself and the world around you, enriching your life with a sense of purpose and fulfillment.

To seamlessly weave somatic practices into your lifestyle, you can consider various strategies. For instance, dedicating specific times each day for somatic exercises like morning meditation or evening yoga helps cultivate a regular practice habit. Consistency is key to reaping the full benefits of somatic practices.

Exploring a wide array of somatic practices allows you to find those that resonate with you personally, ensuring your routine stays engaging and addresses various aspects of your well-being. Experimenting with different techniques helps you discover what works best for you.

Additionally, integrating mindfulness and body awareness into daily activities enhances the effectiveness and applicability of your practice. Whether it's practicing mindful eating, incorporating mindful walking into your daily commute, or simply taking moments throughout the day to check in with your body and breath, every opportunity for mindfulness strengthens your somatic awareness.

Furthermore, joining classes or groups can provide motivation and a sense of belonging, enriching your somatic experience through shared learning and support. Connecting with others on a similar journey can inspire you to stay committed to your practice and deepen your understanding of somatic principles.

Lastly, investing time in learning about somatic theories and techniques and engaging in reflective practices deepens your appreciation and understanding of their benefits. Reading books, attending workshops, or seeking guidance from experienced practitioners offer valuable insights and support your ongoing growth and development.

By incorporating these strategies into your life, you can cultivate a more holistic approach to well-being, one that nurtures harmony between mind, body, and spirit. As you continue on your somatic journey, let us remember that each step you take, no matter how small, brings you closer to a life of greater balance, resilience, and fulfillment.

In conclusion, *Somatic Therapy 101* has been more than just a guidebook—it has been a companion on your journey toward self-discovery and healing. Through its pages, you've explored the depths of the mind-body connection, unlocking insights and practices that have the power to transform your life. Let's reflect on the lessons learned and the wisdom gained, knowing that the path ahead is illuminated by infinite possibilities.

Thank you for joining in on this transformative odyssey through the realm of somatic therapy. Your commitment to your well-being is a testament to the resilience of the human spirit and the power of self-care. As we move forward, may we continue to embrace the journey with open hearts and open minds, ever grateful for the opportunity to cultivate a life of greater health, happiness, and fulfillment.

As we conclude our exploration of this book, if you would be so kind as to share your reflections on this book, it would be greatly appreciated. Your insights are invaluable as we strive to provide resources and support for your somatic journey. Please consider leaving a review and sharing your experiences with others who may benefit from this transformative journey.

Thank you once again for your dedication and commitment to your well-being. I would also like to introduce the next book in this series, *Somatic Therapy 201: Dive Deeper into the Mind-Body Connection with Advanced Tools to Master Self-Discovery and Growth.*

May your somatic journey continue to unfold with grace and wisdom, guiding you toward a life of profound healing and fulfillment.

Keeping the Game Alive

Congratulations on completing *Somatic Therapy 101: An Interactive Guide to Alleviate Stress, Overcome Deep-Rooted Trauma, and Strengthen the Mind-Body Connection with Easy Tools and Exercises.* By now, you've taken significant steps toward understanding and lightening the load of life's challenges. You've learned not just to carry your rocks, but how to set them down gently and walk forward with ease.

Now that you're equipped with the knowledge and tools to face life's stresses and traumas with a renewed sense of strength and clarity, it's time to share this gift. Just as you've discovered ways to reconnect with the beauty of your journey, you have the power to guide others to the same path of healing and self-discovery.

Imagine the difference we can make together if every reader took a moment to share their experience. Your insights and break-throughs can light the way for someone else who is still navigating their journey. Here's how you can keep the game alive:

Share Your Journey

Your journey doesn't end here. It's a continuing process of growth, learning, and sharing. Take a moment to reflect on your experience with the book and how it has impacted your life. Then, consider sharing your story in a review.

Leave a Review

A few words from you can illuminate the path for others. By leaving a review, you're not just sharing your opinion; you're offering hope and guidance to those still searching for a way to lighten their load. Your review can point them toward the tools and exercises that have helped you reconnect with yourself and the world around you.

Here's how to leave your review:

Simply scan the QR code below or follow this link to share your thoughts:

https://www.amazon.com/review/create-review/?
asin=B0D2NNZPGM

Spread the Word

If this book has opened new doors for you, consider sharing it with friends, family, or anyone who might benefit from its lessons. Your recommendation could be the key that unlocks someone else's journey towards healing and growth.

Join the Community

Remember, you're not alone on this path. By sharing your experiences and supporting each other, we create a community of learners and healers, all dedicated to finding and maintaining balance in our lives. Connect with like-minded individuals who are on a similar path of growth and self-discovery. Feel free to join our vibrant Facebook community! Simply scan the QR code below to become part of a supportive network where insights, stories, and encouragement flow freely.

Thank you for being a part of this journey. Your willingness to share your experience and pass on the knowledge you've gained is what keeps the game alive. Together, we can continue to grow, heal, and help others do the same.

- With gratitude, Lizanne Douglas

P.S. - Every review, every shared story, and every recommendation helps to build a network of support and understanding. Thank you for contributing to this community and for helping to spread the transformative power of somatic therapy. Let's keep the game alive, together.

REFERENCES

A Holistic Path to healing: somatic therapy. (2023, January 2). Meridian University. https://meridianuniversity.edu/content/a-holistic-path-to-healing-somatic-therapy

Araminta. (2022, February 16). *5 Benefits of Somatic Therapy - Khiron Clinics.* Khiron Clinics. https://khironclinics.com/blog/5-benefits-of-somatic-therapy/

Aybar, S. (2021, July 21). *4 Somatic Therapy Exercises for Healing from Trauma.* Psych Central. https://psychcentral.com/lib/somatic-therapy-exercises-for-trauma

Benjamin, R. (2023, August 17). The 5 Levels of Self- and Body-Awareness, and How to know where You're at. *Medium.* https://betterhumans.pub/the-5-levels-of-self-and-body-awareness-and-how-to-know-where-youre-at-c3379e9af072

BetterHelp Editorial Team. (2023, December 6). *A guide: What is somatic therapy?* https://www.betterhelp.com/advice/therapy/what-is-somatic-therapy-and-how-does-it-work/

Bhandari, T. (2023, April 20). *Mind-body connection is built into brain, study suggests | Washington University School of Medicine in St. Louis.* Washington University School of Medicine in St. Louis. https://medicine.wustl.edu/news/mind-body-connection-is-built-into-brain-study-suggests/

Blackstone, M. (2023, February 23). How to develop body awareness as an Adult - EMPOWER YOURWELLNESS. *EMPOWER YOURWELLNESS.* https://www.empoweryourwellness.online/improve-your-body-awareness-for-injury-prevention/

Breen, M. (2023, September 15). *What is the Difference Between Somatic Therapy and Talk Therapy? — Repose.* Repose. https://byrepose.com/journal/what-is-the-difference-between-somatic-therapy-and-talk-therapy

Canonico, M. (2021, August 7). *Understanding how trauma affects health and health care - CHCS blog.* Center for Health Care Strategies. https://www.chcs.org/understanding-trauma-affects-health-health-care/

Celestine, N., PhD. (2024, February 29). *What is mindful breathing? Exercises, scripts, and videos.* PositivePsychology.com. https://positivepsychology.com/mindful-breathing/

Chalicha, E., Akuretiya, S., & Ghiur, T. (2023, December 17). *10 Somatic exercises to release Pent-Up emotions.* BetterMe Blog. https://betterme.world/articles/somatic-exercises/

Chapter 3 Understanding the Impact of Trauma. (n.d.). National Library of Medicine. https://www.ncbi.nlm.nih.gov/books/NBK207191/

Clark-Jones, T. (2023, June 23). *Stress less with mindful walking.* Michigan Sate University. https://www.thelancet.com/action/doSearch?type=quicksearch& text1=case+study+somatic+therapy&field1=AllField&journalCode= lanpsy&SeriesKey=lanpsy

Clinic, C. (2023, December 6). *What happens to your body during the Fight-or-Flight response?* Cleveland Clinic. https://health.clevelandclinic.org/what-happens-to-your-body-during-the-fight-or-flight-response/

Delaney, J. (2023, April 19). *Why Body Awareness is Key to Emotional Regulation.* Positive Pranic. https://positivepranic.com/why-body-awareness-is-key-to-emotional-regulation-how-body-scan-meditation-can-help-you-manage-diffi cult-emotions/

Eightify. (2023, September 27). *15-Minute morning somatic routine for a refreshed start.* Eightify Youtube Summaries. https://eightify.app/summary/health-and-wellness/15-minute-morning-somatic-routine-for-a-refreshed-start

Erica Webb SelfKind Yoga and Pilates. (2022, November 9). *Somatic Yoga for bedtime and sleep* [Video]. YouTube. https://www.youtube.com/watch? v=TAajaRtxxWw

Fox, S. M. (2021, February 27). *What is Somatic Self Care? | Stephanie Mara.* Stephanie Mara. https://www.stephaniemara.com/blog/what-is-somatic-self-care

Fritscher, L. (2023, October 23). *What is object relations theory?* Verywell Mind. https://www.verywellmind.com/what-is-object-relations-theory-2671995

Fulcher, M. (2020). *An Exploration of the evolution of somatic therapists as it pertains to mindfulness-based somatic therapy as a trauma treatment.* https://core.ac.uk/down load/pdf/322795287.pdf

Gemma. (2023, August 4). *What is trauma Sensitive yoga? + Common Trauma Informed Yoga poses | The Yogatique.* The Yogatique. https://theyogatique.com/ what-is-trauma-informed-yoga/

Gestalt therapy and focusing. (n.d.). https://healingrefuge.com/approaches/gestalt-therapy-and-focusing/

Glavan, M. (2021, April 29). *Incorporating Somatic Practices and theory on the high school dance team.* https://liberalarts.tulane.edu/sites/default/files/sites/ default/files/6531/Guest%20-%20Incorporating%20Somatic%20Practices% 20and%20Theory.pdf

Goldstein, E. (2023, November 8). *10 Somatic interventions explained — Integrative Psychotherapy Mental Health blog.* Integrative Psychotherapy & Trauma Treatment. https://integrativepsych.co/new-blog/somatic-therapy-explained-methods

GoodTherapy Editor Team. (2016, May 9). *Object relations.* https://www.goodther apy.org/learn-about-therapy/types/object-relations

Grothe, T. (2023, October 31). *Easy somatic exercises for kids and adults to try together.* Parents. https://www.parents.com/somatic-exercises-for-kids-and-adults-8367337

Hadley, H., & Hadley, H. (2018, October 10). *The Power of Somatics before Sleep | Total Somatics.* Total Somatics. https://totalsomatics.com/the-power-of-somat ics-before-sleep/

Harvard Health. (2020, July 6). *Understanding the stress response.* https://www. health.harvard.edu/staying-healthy/understanding-the-stress-response

Hoshaw, C. (2021, February 26). *Body Awareness: How to Deepen Your Connection with Your Body.* Healthline.

How to Manage Trauma. (n.d.). https://www.thenationalcouncil.org/wp-content/ uploads/2022/08/Trauma-infographic.pdf

Kalinda Kano. (2018, May 11). *TRE, Trauma releasing Exercises* [Video]. YouTube. https://www.youtube.com/watch?v=26zoFKZzbQc

Lebow, H. I. (2023, January 21). *How does your body remember trauma?* Psych Central. https://psychcentral.com/health/how-your-body-remembers-trauma

Leonard, J. (2020, June 3). *What is trauma? What to know.* https://www.medicalnew stoday.com/articles/trauma

https://www.healthline.com/health/mind-body/body-awareness\

Lpc, J. B. M. (2017, June 17). *Acceptance and Commitment therapy technique: the observing self.* Psych Central. https://psychcentral.com/pro/psychoeducation/ 2017/06/acceptance-and-commitment-therapy-technique-the-observing-self

McDonnell, C. (2020, November 13). Making Somatics part of your routine – Part 1 - Learn Somatics. *Learn Somatics.* https://learnsomatics.ie/making-somatics-part-of-your-routine-part-1/

Meehan, E., & Carter, B. (2021). Moving with Pain: Principles from the somatic practices can offer to people living with chronic pain. *National Library of Medicine.* https://www.ncbi.nlm.nih.gov/pmc/articles/PMC7868595/

Meyer, L., M. S. (2021, September 24). *5 Mindful Steps for Self-Observation.* Psychology Today. https://www.psychologytoday.com/us/blog/mindful-recov ery/202109/5-mindful-steps-self-observation

MindTools | Home. (n.d.). https://www.mindtools.com/aul3lwx/guided-imagery

National Science Foundation. (2023, May 23). Mind-body connection is built into brain, study suggests. *NSF - National Science Foundation.* https://new.nsf.gov/ news/mind-body-connection-built-brain-study-suggests

Nunez, K. (2020, September 10). *The benefits of guided imagery and how to do it.* Healthline. https://www.healthline.com/health/guided-imagery

Pedersen, T. (2021, August 18). *All about somatic therapy.* Psych Central. https://

psychcentral.com/blog/how-somatic-therapy-can-help-patients-suffering-from-psychological-trauma

Perishable. (2024, February 20). *SE 101 - Somatic Experiencing® International*. Somatic Experiencing® International. https://traumahealing.org/se-101/

Physiology of Stress and its Management. (n.d.). https://www.heraldopenaccess.us/openaccess/physiology-of-stress-and-its-management

Physical Symptoms of Emotional Distress: Somatic Symptoms and Related Disorders. (2023, October). American Academy of Child and Adolescent Psychiatry. https://www.aacap.org/AACAP/Families_and_Youth/Facts_for_Families/FFF-Guide/Physical_Symptoms_of_Emotional_Distress-Somatic_Symptoms_and_Related_Disorders-124.aspx

Price, C., & Hooven, C. (2017). Interoceptive Awareness Skills for Emotion Regulation: Theory and Approach of Mindful Awareness in Body-Oriented Therapy. *National Library of Medicine*. https://www.ncbi.nlm.nih.gov/pmc/articles/PMC5985305/

Price, C., & Hooven, C. (2018). Interoceptive Awareness Skills for Emotion Regulation: Theory and Approach of Mindful Awareness in Body-Oriented Therapy (MABT). *Frontiers in Psychology, 9*. https://doi.org/10.3389/fpsyg.2018.00798

Professional, C. C. M. (n.d.). *Stress*. Cleveland Clinic. https://my.clevelandclinic.org/health/articles/11874-stress

Quinn, D. (2023, May 25). *Somatic Therapy: Understanding the Mind-Body connection*. Sandstone Care. https://www.sandstonecare.com/blog/somatic-therapy/

Relational Somatic Psychotherapy. (2018, October 25). The Association of Former Students. https://www.aggienetwork.com/news/149915/relational-somatic-psychotherapy/

Rice, A. (2022, January 4). *Trauma-Informed Yoga: a guide*. Psych Central. https://psychcentral.com/health/what-is-trauma-informed-yoga

Richmond, C. (2018, December 10). *Emotional trauma and the Mind-Body connection*. WebMD. https://www.webmd.com/mental-health/features/emotional-trauma-mind-body-connection

Ryt, M. B. P. D. (2023, April 2). *Home page - EMPOWER YOURWELLNESS*. EMPOWER YOURWELLNESS. https://www.empoweryourwellness.online/improve-your-body-awareness-for-injury-prevention/BD8&alloworigin=1&disposition=0

Seaver, M. (2023, March 30). *5 mindfulness breathing exercises you can do anywhere, anytime*. Real Simple. https://www.realsimple.com/health/mind-mood/breathing-exercises

Sep, R. K. L. (2023, October 18). *5 Somatic Experiencing techniques that anyone can use to stay grounded*. Life Care Wellness. https://life-care-wellness.com/5-somatic-experiencing-techniques-that-anyone-can-use-to-stay-grounded/

Shane, P. (1987). Gestalt Review. *Gestalt Institute of Clevland for Its Members, II*(1). https://static1.squarespace.com/static/572d003b40261d2ef97e5b0b/t/5b0ec25d6d2a73f6c9201895/1527693919287/1987+Gestalt+Review+Vol+2+No+1.pdf

Somatic Awareness: the science of connecting mind and body. (n.d.). https://www.brainfirsttraininginstitute.com/blog/somatic-awareness-the-science-of-connecting-mind-and-body

Somatic Psychology: Meaning and origins. (2022, November 22). Meridian University. https://meridianuniversity.edu/content/somatic-psychology-meaning-and-origins

Somatic Therapy. (n.d.). Psychology Today. https://www.psychologytoday.com/us/therapy-types/somatic-therapy

Stone, R. (2022, September 23). *Somatic Techniques for Stress and Anxiety — Brooklyn Somatic Therapy.* Brooklyn Somatic Therapy. https://www.brooklynsomatictherapy.com/blog/somatic-techniques-for-stress-and-anxiety

Stress Assessment/ Stress Management Checklist. (n.d.). https://www.covenantcc.co/sovlib/external_articles/stress_assessment_management_checklist.pdf

Stress Symptom Checklist. (n.d.). https://www.baylor.edu/content/services/document.php/183434.pdf

Stress symptoms: Effects of stress on the body. (n.d.). WebMD. https://www.webmd.com/balance/stress-management/stress-symptoms-effects_of-stress-on-the-body

Signs and symptoms of stress. (n.d.). Mind. https://www.mind.org.uk/information-support/types-of-mental-health-problems/stress/signs-and-symptoms-of-stress/

Talks, R. C. (n.d.). *The impacts of stress on your mental health.* Red Cross Canada. https://www.redcross.ca/blog/2020/10/the-impact-of-stress-on-your-mental-health

Talk Therapy vs. Somatic Therapy: Key Differences. (n.d.). Beat Anxiety Feel to Heal. https://beatanxiety.me/talk-therapy-vs-somatic-therapy-key-differences/

TemplateLab. (2021, August 18). *25 Printable Daily Planner Templates (FREE in Word/Excel/PDF).* TemplateLab. https://templatelab.com/daily-planner-template/

The benefits of somatic therapy (Talk therapy isn't your only option!) | Nivati. (n.d.). https://nivati.com/blog/the-benefits-of-somatic-therapy-talk-therapy-isnt-your-only-option

The Lancet Psychiatry. https://www.thelancet.com/action/doSearch?type=quick

search&text1=case+study+somatic+therapy&field1=AllField&journalCode=
lanpsy&SeriesKey=lanpsy

Toussaint, L., Nguyen, Q., Roettger, C., Dixon, K., Offenbacher, M., Kohls, N., Hirsch, J., & Sirois, F. (2021, July 2). *Effectiveness of Progressive Muscle Relaxation, Deep Breathing and Guided Imagery in Promoting Pschological and Physiological States of Relaxtion.* National Library of Medicine. https://www.ncbi.nlm.nih. gov/pmc/articles/PMC8272667/

Trauma. (n.d.). https://www.apa.org. https://www.apa.org/topics/trauma

Trauma Sensitive Yoga - 14 Precautions to Keep in Mind when Teaching | Tummee.com Trusted by Yoga Therapists. (n.d.). https://www.tummee.com/yoga-therapy/ trauma-sensitive-yoga

TRE (Trauma Release Exercises). (n.d.). Osteopathy for All. https://osteopathyforall. co.uk/toolkits/mindbody-toolkit/trauma-release-exercises/

Warren, S. (2019, June 26). *How to get the most out of Clinical Somatics exercises.* Somatic Movement Center. https://somaticmovementcenter.com/somatic-exercises-learn-hanna-somatic-exercises/

Weber, M. (2023, October 4). EMDR Therapy Helped Me Heal from Trauma. Now I Use it to Help My Clients. *HealthyWomen.* https://www.healthywomen.org/ real-women-real-stories/emdr-therapy-helped-me-heal-from-trauma-now-i-use-it-to-help-my-clients

Whaley, M., LCSW. (2007, December). *How the Physiology of Somatic Experiencing can give the Gestalt therapist a broader understanding of what they are already doing and allow them to do it better.* http://nebula.wsimg.com/f2ee75cdb1029bae6fd cbf4474d5c692?AccessKeyId=110A682CAE49E5C1ABD8&alloworigin=1& disposition=0

What's the difference between mental and physical stress? (2015, January 28). Physics Forums: Science Discussion, Homework Help, Articles. https://www.physicsfo rums.com/threads/whats-the-difference-between-mental-and-physical-stress. 794754/

Wong, A., PhD. (2023, June 2). *Finding Freedom from Anxiety: Somatic Tools for Managing Stress.* Somatopia. https://www.somatopia.com/blog/somatic-ther apy-anxiety-stress

Wright, M. (2022, January 27). *The Importance of Body Awareness — Holistic and Somatic therapy | Berkeley & Richmond.* Holistic and Somatic Therapy | Berkeley & Richmond. https://www.lifebydesigntherapy.com/blog/why-it-is-impor tant-to-have-body-awareness/10/2019

Yanay-Triner, M. (2023, March 13). *How to incorporate somatic practices into your daily life - Marina Yanay-Triner Coaching.* Marina Yanay-Triner Coaching. https://marinayt.com/how-to-incorporate-somatic-practices/

Yoga | Pilates | Tai-Chi - Wantagh, NY. (n.d.). https://www.harmonyyogaandwellness.com/

Made in the USA
Las Vegas, NV
16 September 2024

95320644R00118